THAT'S THE STUFF, KID

The Life and Times of Baseball Legend Stuffy McInnis

FAMOUS FEATS

SECOND SERIES

First baseman Stuffy McInnis fielded .999 in 1921 (1 error)

29 ©1980 R.G. Laughlin

By Edward R. Brown

THAT'S THE STUFF, KID

The Life And Times Of Baseball Legend Stuffy McInnis

A Beverly Historical Society Publication
117 Cabot St
Beverly, Massachusetts 01915-5196
www.beverlyhistory.org

ISBN 978-1-891906-02-2

Cover Illustration: This 1980 cartoon from the R. G. Laughlin "Famous Feats" series celebrates Stuffy's almost perfect fielding record in 1921, when he played for the Red Sox, not the Athletics. (Beverly Historical Society)

Cover and book design: Edward McFadden

Editor: Terri McFadden

Dedication:

For my father, Edward Lyman Brown, Jr., who introduced me to baseball many decades ago; to everyone who has played, coached, organized, or enjoyed watching this great American game that unites the generations; and to those whose hard work made possible the Harry Ball Field Little League complex in Beverly, Massachusetts.

CONTENTS

INTRODUCTION

He was born in the North Shore fishing community of Gloucester, Mass. and lived the better part of his life in nearby Manchester, which in his day was plain Manchester, without the "By-the-Sea" affectation, which the town adopted in recent years. He is undoubtedly one of the 10 greatest major league baseball players to be overlooked for admission to baseball's Hall of Fame – a .307 lifetime batter over an 18-year big league career, who was even better known for his defensive prowess as a first baseman. He long held the record for consecutive fielding chances without an error, despite the fact that at 5 feet 8 inches tall he was unusually small for his position. In an era when professional baseball was often known for cutthroat competition, he was considered a gentleman, even though he may have been the only player in major league history to steal first base (along with second, third and home), by cleverly taking advantage of a short-lived rule change to flummox the 1911 Boston Red Sox. He played in five World Series, three times for Connie Mack's Philadelphia Athletics, for the Boston Red Sox in the famous 1918 classic that was Boston's last world championship until 2004, and finally for the Pittsburgh Pirates in 1925. Perhaps the fact that he batted only .200 in those five fall classics combined, along with his shortage of home run power, worked against him in the Hall of Fame balloting. Later in life he coached three New England college baseball teams, including Harvard's. In addition to his baseball skills he was a formidable golfer who still holds the course record at the Candlewood Golf Club in Ipswich, which he set nearly seven decades ago.

But if John "Stuffy" McInnis hadn't joined an independent, semi-pro ball club in Beverly, Mass. as a teenager, he might never have been discovered and signed by the legendary Connie Mack, manager and part owner of the Philadelphia (now Oakland) Athletics for the first half of the 20th century. It was the Beverly team's field boss, the somewhat mysterious T. Richard "Dick" Madden, who recommended to Mack in 1908 that he sign the diminutive youngster, who was the toast of the Beverly fans in the last season for the local team and its ballpark. That ballpark, known as Peabody's Field, near the Montserrat train station, was turned into a housing development in the spring of 1909 after Beverly city fathers muffed their chance to acquire it for a proposed public showplace. It is almost certain that those same rabid Beverly fans gave McInnis his lifetime nickname. We know from Beverly newspaper accounts that young Jack was being referred to as Stuffy as early as 1907, when he was just 16. A biographical note says he gained the appellation as a teen in the "Boston suburban leagues." When the youth would turn another of his spectacular plays, usually at shortstop, sometimes in the outfield for the Madden team, appreciative fans shouted from the grandstand, "That's the stuff, kid!" It wasn't long until everyone started referring to young Jack as Stuffy. Whether this first happened in Beverly or not, it was in Beverly that the nickname became permanently attached to the popular young player. And after a quick detour to Haverhill in the late summer of 1908, Stuffy McInnis was on his way to baseball's big time. There he would make his mark, season after season.

(The author would like to thank John C. "Finney" Burke and Constance "Connie" Brown, who remember Stuffy well, for sharing memories; Mary Mahoney, Stuffy's grandson Richard Littlefield, Mike at the Manchester Public Library, Tim McInnis (no relation to Stuffy), Ed McFadden, and my Beverly Historical Society colleagues, Sue Goganian, Darren Brown, Terri McFadden, and Jeff Dauzat for their support; and Art Edwards, who back in 1999 first called my attention to Stuffy McInnis's Beverly connection).

A BOY'S QUICK JOURNEY: GLOUCESTER TO BEVERLY TO THE SHOW

"That durned kid will be a great player when he grows big!"

   – *'Cuban Giant' Satterfield to Beverly fans about 16-year-old Stuffy, July 4, 1907*

John Phalen McInnis was born in Gloucester, Mass. on Sept. 19, 1890, the second youngest of five sons of Stephen and Udavilla (Grady) McInnis. His parents' names connoted good Irish stock, but the McInnises seem to have come to Gloucester from Nova Scotia. The mother's rather unusual first name is also a surname known in the Canadian province in the 19th century, but an on-line search for the parents' birth records came up empty.

Stephen McInnis seems to have been a hard working husband and father who was employed as caretaker of a Gloucester stable and also drove a team of horses. With the appearance of the gasoline powered "horseless carriage," Stephen McInnis learned to drive a car and worked as a chauffeur. In addition, he served his community as a call fireman. Up until the 1960s, before the term "firefighter" replaced fireman, larger

3

communities such as Gloucester relied on call men to supplement the full timers on the fire department. (Many smaller towns still are served largely by a call force.) The call men, who were paid either an annual stipend or by the hour, usually had jobs in town and so were able to turn out whenever they were summoned by the blasts of the alarm horns atop the various fire stations.

According to Aaron Davis and Paul Rogers III, writing for the Baseball Biography Project, all five of the McInnis boys enjoyed playing the game, which had become a national mania. But it was little Jack who, despite his small stature, soon established himself as the best baseball player in the family and in the town. There were of course no formal youth leagues then, and no money for real equipment, but before he reached his teens young Jack was able to hold his own on the ball field with older boys in Gloucester pickup games. Thinking back on those glorious boyhood days, Stuffy had this recollection for *Harvard Crimson* writer Stephen N. Cady in 1949: "Just as soon as the snow was off the streets, we'd be out playing under the (street) lights with a yarn ball our mothers would knit for us. When we knocked the yarn apart, we'd pull it back together with black tape." In 1906, at 15, he led the Gloucester High School nine to a championship season. High school baseball, with its weekday afternoon contests, didn't draw huge crowds, but the youngster's performance was enough to attract the attention of Dick Madden, the leading baseball promoter in nearby Beverly, nine miles down the North Shore coast. Although the boy was only 16 that spring, Madden offered Jack McInnis a chance to join his highly respected ball club, which played an independent schedule against all opponents that Madden could line up, for the 1907 season. For the most part, the Beverly team, which seems to have had no formal nickname, was a mixture of collegians and a few older men, with the occasional "ringer" (undoubtedly paid for the day) brought in to bolster the lineup for an important game. Obviously with the approval of his parents, the lad accepted the invitation. From all that can be learned, bolstered by what was written in his hometown obituary, he left Gloucester High School prior to graduation to pursue his love of and obvious talent for baseball.

T. Richard "Dick" Madden, who managed Beverly's semi-pro baseball team in the early years of the 20th century, is a somewhat mysterious figure today. Contemporary accounts in the *Beverly Evening Times* referred to him only as "Manager Madden," but the weekly *Saturday Evening Citizen* of Aug. 15, 1908 calls him 'T. R. Madden." Beverly's only Madden family of the time lived at 44 Wallis St. in downtown Beverly.

The father, Thomas E. Madden was, according to the 1908 Beverly City Directory, a section foreman for the Boston and Maine Railroad, which in the 1890s had acquired the Eastern Railroad, the line that brought the "iron horse" to the North Shore in the late 1830s and the 1840s. Living at home then were two sons, William, also employed by the railroad as a section hand, and T. Richard, whose occupation was listed as "clerk, Boston." In 1893, T. Richard Madden was employed as a mail messenger at the Beverly Post Office, but by 1897 he was listed as a student. In 1903 he was a clerk at an unspecified Boston firm. From later information it can be learned that Madden was an early associate of the Submarine Signal Company, a pioneer company formed in Boston in 1901 with offices on State Street and laboratories on Atlantic Avenue. It was the first commercial enterprise to conduct underwater sound research and build equipment to improve navigational safety. It became the main sonar supplier to the U.S. Navy, and in 1946 was merged into Raytheon Corp. Madden's baseball team was gone before the 1909 season, for reasons which will be examined in an appendix to this account, but his occupation remained the same for several years thereafter. Then in 1915 came the strangest entry of all, "Removed to London, England." That move can be understood, however, after reading that Madden had embarked seven years earlier on a business voyage aboard the *Lusitania* with top officials of Submarine Signal, which established a London office. To remove any further doubt, an article by Gary Frost Lewis in the July 2001 issue of "Technology and Culture," a publication of John's Hopkins University, telling of Reginald Fessenden, inventor of the Fessenden Oscillator which was used by Submarine Signal Co., references a Nov. 1, 1913 letter to Fessenden from T. Richard Madden.

Madden's team played its home games at Peabody's Field, located between Essex Street and Odell Avenue near the Montserrat railroad station, which before 1909 was just a flag stop for the trains. The property was owned by the Prospect Hill Syndicate, whose trustee, Henry W. Peabody, built "Parramatta," off Corning Street, for his summer home. That estate became the second summer White House for President William Howard Taft in 1911-12, after Maria Antoinette Evans "evicted" the president and his family from their first summer digs at what is now Beverly's Lynch Park. Peabody, either personally or through the real estate trusts he controlled, owned large chunks of Beverly real estate. He had constructed housing developments on Prospect Hill and on the opposite (east) side of Essex Street. But the 13-acre tract bounded by Spring, Odell, Essex and Baker Avenue still was vacant space, and

Henry Peabody generously allowed Beverly to build a baseball park there, with the expressed hope that the city would acquire permanent ownership. While we have no photographic evidence of Peabody's Field, the 1907 assessors' map in the collection of the Beverly Historical Society shows a rectangular structure labeled "grand stand" on the Odell Avenue side of the property. Madden's team often drew sizeable crowds, and an advertisement in the Times reveals that 25 cents admission was charged per game, which amounted to an hour's pay for a working man in those days. Fans who wanted a reserved seat in the grandstand had to fork over ten cents extra. There must have been a fence around the field with a gate in order to control admission. In addition to baseball games, an early version of the "Sam-Sam" carnival – first sponsored by the Union Club of Beverly before being taken over by the United Shoe Machinery Corporation -- took place at Peabody's Field. The United Shoe and Beverly High School baseball teams also used Peabody's Field. If an undated and unlabeled photograph of a Beverly baseball team of the time in the Historical Society files, obviously a men's team, was indeed the Madden nine, the manager, standing in the middle of the second row, was a stocky man wearing a baseball cap and jacket. Standing next to the dapper "civilian" at the end of the second row is what appears to be the team's youngest member, a short, slender lad who bears a striking resemblance to the face of "McInnes (sic), s.s., Phila. Amer." on the 1909 baseball card issued by the American Caramel Co. for a rookie major league infielder. Box scores show that Madden himself played centerfield until 1906, after which he became strictly a bench manager.

We can't positively say just when Jack McInnis came by the nickname "Stuffy" that remained his moniker on and off the baseball field for the rest of his life, but it likely occurred when he was a 16-year-old sensation playing for the Beverly baseball club. Some biographical accounts say it happened while he was playing as a youth in the "Boston suburban leagues," when, after the youngster made a sensational defensive play, appreciative spectators and teammates hollered, "That's the stuff, kid!" Soon he was being called "Stuffy" by everyone. Even if the tag was first applied by older boys when McInnis was learning his way around the game as a child in Gloucester, there can be no doubt that the enthusiastic supporters of Dick Madden's Beverly baseball club perfected the nickname and made it stick. Not only were the Beverly fans willing to pay the price of admission to games at Peabody's Field, many also followed the local club on the road.

Stuffy joined Madden's team in the spring of 1907. Despite the lack of formal league affiliation, interest in the Beverly ball team was running high as the chill of winter gave way to warmer days that year. An early May story in the *Beverly Evening Times* headlined "Coming Attractions for Ballplayers" informed fans that "Manager Madden" had just booked games against highly regarded opponents representing Dorchester, Cambridge and "Newtowne." But the real excitement came a few days later when the Times revealed that the manager of the Wakefield men's team had issued a challenge to Beverly to play a best-of-seven series to determine what was to be called "The Championship of the State." Obviously Bishop, the Wakefield manager, believed that his team and Madden's were the best amateur ball clubs around, and that the winner of the series could rightfully lay claim to the mythical title. On May 14 the *Times* reported that Beverly had accepted the Rattan Towners' challenge, and that Madden and Bishop were to meet that night in Salem to work out the details for the series. So hot was baseball excitement in 1907 Beverly that the Rev. E. A. Hoyt, pastor of the Universalist Church, preached a sermon that summer entitled "The Game of Baseball and the Game of Life."

Meanwhile young Mr. McInnis made his debut in a Beverly uniform, performing in right field and at second base as the team's youngest member. On Saturday, May 18, Stuffy was in the starting lineup at second base, batting eighth, had a hit and scored a run as Beverly posted a 12-5 triumph over "Newtowne" in front of an enthusiastic throng at Peabody's Field. ("Newtowne was easy," the *Times* sniffed.) But it was the kid's defensive work that really stirred the crowd, and could well have put the exclamation point on the youngster's nickname. The *Times* writer exulted: "McInnis played a snappy game at Matthews' old position at second, getting five assists and a putout with a clean record." With the regular catcher missing that day, Matthews had switched from his normal position to take over behind the plate. On Memorial Day, the Madden men hosted both Neponset/Dorchester and Wellington (Medford) for a doubleheader. With Matthews back at second base, McInnis played right field in both games as Beverly treated the home crowd to a pair of easy wins, blanking Dorchester 8-0 in the morning game and topping Wellington 9-4 in the afternoon. Bill Matthews, we would later learn, was a Harvard Law School student, as were Beverly teammates Eddie Loughlin and Eddie Grant.

The lad's nickname also began to make it into print. After a June 9 contest, McInnis was referred to as "Stubby." That might either have been a mistake by the writer who misunderstood what was being yelled out to the diminutive young star, or it could even have been changed by the typesetter who thought that "Stuffy" couldn't be right. But in the write-up of a game against Salem, things were crystal clear. *Times* readers were told how the Beverly right fielder was robbed of a hit by Kiley, the Salem third baseman, who "made a grand stop of McInnis' hard daisy cutter" (then a slang term for a well struck ground ball.) His throw to first was a bit low, but it snuffed out 'Stuffy' all right."

Meanwhile, the first of June brought the start of the long anticipated "championship" series with Wakefield, which would carry over into July as games were scheduled around the two teams' other commitments. A big crowd turned out for the opener at Peabody's Field, but the local fans went home disappointed as Harris, the Rattan Towners' ace pitcher, shut down the Madden team, 4-1. (Wakefield's nickname came from its fame as the town in which the wicker 'rattan' furniture developed by old Cyrus Wakefield was assembled.) Stuffy played second base that day, but was back in right field the following Saturday, when Beverly traveled to Wakefield for game two and evened the series by winning a 1-0 pitchers duel. The evenly matched teams also split the next two games, with Stuffy playing right field. *Times* readers were informed that "McInnis also contributed a great catch in the 7th inning" of a 4-1 Beverly victory.

By the fifth game, to be played in Wakefield on Saturday, June 22, interest had reached such a fever pitch that Madden made arrangements for a special train to carry Beverly fans to the game, ensuring a large visitors' cheering section. It should be remembered that the manager's father was a railroad foreman, which might have facilitated the arrangements. The special train was to leave Beverly Depot at 2:15. Since Beverly and Wakefield are on different rail lines then and now, it seems impossible today to imagine a train connecting the two places without a lot of time-consuming backing and switching at Boston. But in those days it could be done, thanks to the "high car line." When the original Salem tunnel was constructed under Washington Street, the low bore could accommodate the freight cars of the day. But by the turn of the century, taller cars were being built and some of them wouldn't fit through the tunnel. To accommodate freight destined for Eastern Route points north of Salem, the Boston & Maine instituted what was called the "High Car Job." That train departed Boston's freight yard on the Haverhill line, diverted at Wakefield Jct., and proceeded through Lynnfield and West Peabody to a connecting track that paralleled Lowell Street and on to Peabody Square. From thence it connected via the

Danvers Branch track to Northey Point, just east of the tunnel beside the Salem engine house, where it rejoined the Eastern Route main, headed for Beverly and beyond. A special passenger train leaving Beverly could be switched off at Northey Point and sent on its way direct to Wakefield Center station. The cars could be placed on a siding in Wakefield and the steam engine unpinned to be serviced and turned, then hooked to the other end for the ride home. Once back in Beverly, the train would be switched to the Beverly yard track and the engine turned on the turntable for the trip back to Boston. Now, Route 128 crosses where the high car line used to be, and part of the right of way has been turned into a bicycle path. The High Car Job continued to operate until the new Salem tunnel was opened in August of 1958.

Unfortunately, the newspaper for Monday, June 24, 1907, is missing from the roll of microfilm at the Beverly Public Library, so we know nothing about how the train trip went, or how many rode the "white flags" special that day. The *Saturday Evening Citizen* for June 29, however, reported that Wakefield defeated Beverly, 9-6. We do know, thanks to Arthur Edwards, grandson of Alwood Brainard "Barney" Edwards who was Madden's statistician, that the series was tied at three games apiece in mid-July. But apparently managers Madden and Bishop were unable to agree on the date and playing site for a seventh and deciding game, since there is no record of it being played. Because the teams were so even, it might have been fair to just call them co-champions of the state. (Arthur Edwards has confirmed that the dapper man in the photo referred to above was not his grandfather.)

Whether the state championship was decided or not, there was plenty of other baseball activity to whet the appetites of local baseball fans that summer, along with a bit of controversy. The Thanksgiving Day football rivalry between Beverly and Salem was just a few years old in 1907, but the neighboring communities were eager to have at it in baseball as well. A series of three games between the Madden men and a team from Salem was arranged. In the first game, as we have seen, Salem's third baseman, Kiley, robbed Stuffy of a hit by snaring his "daisy cutter." For game two, scheduled for July 20, Dick Madden was taking no chances. A century or so ago, the use of "ringers" was common in small town baseball circles. For a big game, one or more outsiders would be brought in to bolster the home town nine, and although those teams were considered amateur, the term "semi-pro" connoted the fact that a team might pay the ringer for his temporary services. To face Salem, Madden imported one Ira Plank, said by the *Times* to be "an ace from the

Connecticut League" and the younger brother of major league hurler Eddie Plank, to take the mound for Beverly. It paid off, as ringer Plank silenced the Salem bats in a 3-0 Beverly victory, a nine-inning game that took just one hour and 33 minutes to play, typical of the days when ball games were all hustle and no dawdle. The *Citizen* said one thousand fans watched the game at the Bridge Street grounds in Salem, said to be "in terrible shape" since the game was played soon after the annual appearance of the traveling circus. By now, young Stuffy McInnis was so highly regarded that Madden promoted him to the cleanup spot (fourth) in the batting order, and he came through with a base hit. Ira Plank refused to pitch the third and deciding game in the series at Peabody's Field, so Madden called on another import, Sid Hazleton, who was alleged to be from South Framingham. He hurled a two-hit shutout as Beverly (and company) wrapped up the "Essex County Championship" with a 6-0 victory.

But before the third game, a bit of scandal broke forth in the local press with Dick Madden at the center. The *Times* reported that there was talk of a "frame-up" among local ball fans that had nothing to do with the use of imported pitchers. Before the Salem series, a group of backers, presumably including merchants, put together a $100 pot that was to go to the winning team. The scandal involved an allegation that the "management" of the Beverly team also controlled the Salem ball club. In other words, the money was safe no matter who won. Madden declared to the local press "without hesitation" that any claim of him having a financial interest in the Salem club "is a falsehood."

On a happier note, on the Fourth of July in 1907, the Beverly team drew a huge holiday throng to Peabody's Field by booking a game with a barnstorming aggregation known as the Cuban Giants. Despite the name, that team was not from the Caribbean island nation, but rather was made up exclusively of African Americans with names like Smith, Robinson, Brighty and Satterfield. Blacks were banned from major league ball for another 40 years until the Brooklyn Dodgers and Jackie Robinson broke the color line, and the professional Negro Leagues had yet to come into existence. But black ballplayers could and did form traveling teams and were welcome to play exhibitions against small town white opposition, for guaranteed money to cover their expenses. That day would prove a memorable one for Stuffy McInnis, and made a prophet out of one of the visiting black players. Matthews, Beverly's popular second baseman, missed the July 4 game because, as the *Times* reported, it was to be his wedding day. In 1907, that was considered just a barely acceptable excuse to miss a baseball game, and it caused Madden to move Stuffy from right field to fill in again for Matthews at second. The "colored stars" prevailed by a 4-1 score, but it was certainly a day for people to shout, "that's the stuff, kid!" After the little guy robbed Satterfield of a base hit for the second time with a spectacular play, the Cuban Giant jocularly turned to the packed grandstand and bellowed to the local fans some very prophetic words which the *Times* reported: "That durned kid will be a great player when he grows big!"

In 1908, Stuffy, now 17, was back for a second season with the Beverly team, which in one write-up was given the nickname of "Madden's Braves." There was no more right field or second base for the lad, who was written into the lineup at the key position of shortstop, the anchor of the infield. It was evident that he was no longer involved in high school ball in Gloucester, since he was with the Madden team for the season opener on April 20, a bone chilling day on which Beverly whipped a visiting semi-pro team from Woonsocket, R.I. by a 7-1 score. A bit later, on May 9, Stuffy collected two hits in a 7-2 Beverly win over the well-regarded Somerville Braves. Commented the *Beverly Evening Times*: "McInnis was, as usual, there with the goods and delivered them, too. He had two errors but his general play was of the gilt-edged variety." Coming up on the Beverly schedule was a May 17 date with a team from Marlboro, regarded as one of the better baseball towns in eastern Massachusetts. In '08 the *Times* had begun to print a sports column supposedly authored by "F.J. Kanngov," who wrote on May 16: "Stuffy McInnis is stinging the ball right on the nose and fielding his position like a veteran. Save some of those bingles for Marlboro, Stuffy." In a later game versus Hyde Park, the youngster had another memorable day, flawlessly handling six fielding chances at shortstop. The box score that day showed that the rest of the Beverly lineup included the now-married Matthews, Loughlin, Kavanaugh, Burke, Bjorkland, Levins, Conrad, O'Neil, and Blatchford, pitching.

Stuffy went missing from the Beverly lineup for a brief time, when he actually made his professional debut. With Dick Madden's approval, the youthful shortstop agreed to "help out" Billy Hamilton, manager of the Haverhill Hustlers of the Class B New England League (what was Class B then is the equivalent of AA level pro ball today, the second step down from the major leagues). A couple of Hamilton's infielders were temporarily out of action and he needed someone to fill in. Stuffy's reputation obviously had spread to the Merrimack Valley and he would draw pay from Hamilton, who liked what he saw of young Mr. McInnis.

Stuffy soon rejoined his teammates in Beverly, but not for long. Everyone agreed he was getting too good to remain tied to small town ball.

In 1908 there was no word of another challenge from Wakefield and no disputed series with Salem, either. But the Beverly ball club had found a new opponent with which to form a friendly rivalry, the "Townies" from Rockport, who would get together with the Madden men for a series of four summer games that kept the fans buzzing with excitement. They had best enjoy the fun, because although nobody could have guessed it then, by the time the next spring rolled around there would be no Beverly team to root for and no Peabody's Field to play on. For the first game against Rockport, Madden went all out on the ringer route, importing a guy from Wakefield named Leonard to play first base, and benching right fielder Bjorkland in favor of one Cook, said to be "a college man from Pennsylvania." Beverly fans crowded aboard the 3:30 p.m. train to Rockport, where a turnstile count was taken and the attendance was announced as 1,599. For a later game in Beverly against Rockport, Madden jacked up the admission price to 35 cents. With Stuffy playing shortstop and batting cleanup, Beverly gained a split of the first two contests, winning 4-2 at home in the morning and losing 6-5 at Rockport in a twilight rematch the same day, hence the 3:30 train ride.

For the first time, the *Times* threw a bit of criticism Stuffy's way despite the 4-2 win. "McInnis was a bit off in his play the first two innings and the two runs set down to Rockport may be partly charged to him. Sullivan" (Beverly's catcher) "threw down to second to catch a base runner and would have nailed him surely had anyone been there to receive the ball. But Mattie" (meaning Matthews) "was way off second and Stuffy did not wake up to the opportunity, and the ball went cutting the daisies into short center. But the game was won, the fans were pleased and these shortcomings were forgotten." Even 17-year-old baseball heroes can have an occasional defensive lapse. In the third game of the Rockport series, the one at Peabody's Field for which Madden jacked up the admission price by a dime, the home team lost, 8-3, in what the *Times* called "one of the poorest exhibitions of the season." But for Stuffy McInnis, the bright lights of baseball fame were about to be switched on.

On Aug. 6, 1908, a *Times* headline cried out: "Connie Mack To Take McInnis And Martin." We don't know what the relationship was between Dick Madden and Mack, the fabled manager and principal owner of the American League's Philadelphia Athletics. But the account for McInnis in the "Baseball Biography Project" tells us: "On the advice of Dick Madden of the Beverly amateur club – who acted as a scout for the Athletics – McInnis was signed by A's owner-manager Connie Mack at the end of the 1908 season." Madden's occupation was clerk for a Boston firm. When Ban Johnson organized the American League in 1901 as a challenge to the supremacy of the established National League, Mack was one of those who helped put a franchise into Boston, a team first known as the Pilgrims and then the Red Sox. It is possible that Mack and Madden became acquainted at the time, though that is of course mere speculation. At any rate, Mack, who at the same time was launching his Philadelphia Athletics team, obviously knew Madden and trusted his judgment of baseball talent. The *Times* told its readers that both Stuffy and H. Martin, a pitcher, had been recommended to the Athletics by Manager Madden. Since Stuffy was still just 17 in August of 1908, a major league debut would wait until the 1909 season, although Mack was as good as his word. Even then Stuffy, being underage, would not have been allowed to sign a legal document, so his father or another responsible adult would have had to sign for him.

The only possibility for the H. Martin is Harold "Doc" Martin, a Roxbury native who had attended Tufts College. If he was the same Martin who was playing for Beverly at the time, he was being used primarily in center field, but was well regarded as a pro pitching prospect by Dick Madden. The right-hander actually pitched a game for the Philadelphia Athletics early in October of 1908 at age 21, but was blown off the mound in his major league debut. After spending the 1909 and 1910 seasons in the minor leagues, he returned to the A's in 1911, pitching in 11 games, including three starts, while posting a 1-1 record with an earned run average of 4.50. He was released after just two games in 1912, but at least he could always say he had been a part of a world championship team in 1911 and had won a game as a pitcher in the major league. Harold Martin died in Milton, Mass. in 1935 at age 47.

As for Stuffy, he appears to have played his last game for Beverly on Aug. 8 at Rockport, a game in which the *Times* said Rockport was "treated to a coat of whitewash" in a 13-0 romp for the Madden men. The local daily paper was now referring to Stuffy as "Connie Mack's youngest recruit." But since the lad was now bound for the big time, it was decided that he should rejoin Billy Hamilton's Haverhill Hustlers for the remainder of the New England League season. Not only would he be exposed to a faster brand of baseball, the teenager could earn some money from the game he loved, since Hamilton would pay him $100 a month. Stuffy really had little choice, since the Beverly club ended its season early, on Aug. 15 at Wakefield. The *Saturday Evening Citizen* published this tribute to Madden on Aug. 15:

> Beverly has seen its last game on Peabody's field with the old time star lineup of the champions of Essex County, and on Saturday the Beverly team will go to Wakefield for the last game of the summer. Manager T. R. Madden, who has looked after the team since Beverly broke into fast baseball, sails for Europe on Aug. 20 on the *Lusitania* from New York and will be abroad five weeks. He goes with the president of the Submarine Signal Company on a business trip and will visit the foreign cities where the company has interests.
>
> Beverly has seen good ball, fast ball, clean ball and to Madden belongs the credit for this. He has given Beverly a team that has won its way into the front ranks of semi-professional outfits. He has given many men a chance to get into the big leagues, and 'Stuffy' McInnis and Martin who have been signed by 'Connie' Mack are two of the latest to get with the big fellows through the help of the Beverly manager. In the past few years Beverly has played the best teams in the state and some of the fastest out of state, and has won series after series, the last one closing Saturday, won the Essex County championship from Rockport." (It would be nice to know what other players were recommended by Dick Madden.)

When the Hustlers played a doubleheader at Lynn on Aug. 21, Stuffy's friends and admirers from Gloucester and Beverly held "Stuffy McInnis Day" to fete him between the two games. From all accounts, Stuffy acquitted himself very well during his first eight weeks as an outright professional ballplayer, batting .301 in 56 games as an infielder, some at shortstop but mostly at second base, during his two stints with the '08 Hustlers. With a Philadelphia contract in hand for 1909, he then must have spent an anxious winter back in Gloucester, impatiently waiting with nervous anticipation for what the coming spring would have in store for him.

MR. MACK'S FAMOUS $100,000 INFIELD

"It's worth the price of admission to see McInnis play"

— 1912 newspaper clipping quoted by Harvard 'Crimson.' February 1949

"It was almost impossible to hit a ball out of the park in those days. Everything favored the pitchers"

— Stuffy McInnis

S tuffy McInnis must have been nervous indeed in March of 1909 when he reported to the Philadelphia Athletics' spring training camp in the lovely seaside town of Savannah, Georgia. He certainly had never traveled to the South, and despite the confidence in his baseball ability; he was a mere boy among hardened men, professional ballplayers who were known to treat rookies with disdain. Stuffy was not only a rookie, he was only 18, a small town lad with no vices who had spent the previous summer dividing his time between an amateur team and a pro "bush league." One thing that stood in his favor was that his new manager was Connie Mack, who was known for promoting gentlemanly behavior in an era when big league baseball boasted such cutthroat competitors as the Detroit Tigers' ferocious star Ty Cobb. Mack did not smoke or drink alcohol, and it is perhaps telling that his young protégé, Stuffy, was known as a man who lived cleanly all his life. Mack, who managed for half a century wearing a business suit instead of a baseball uniform, also hated the prevalent practice of rattling opponents through "bench jockeying" or yelling insults from the coaching lines. An April 1907 story in the *Beverly Evening Times* headlined "Frowns On Real Noisy Coaching" informed readers that Connie Mack was "not in love with voiced men on the side lines." The Athletics' boss wanted his players and coaches to encourage and assist their own teammates, rather than raining verbal abuse on the opposition.

Stuffy's short stature and youthful appearance must have made him look out of place in the Athletics' camp. According to Davis and Rogers in "The Baseball Biography," the teenager already had run into disrespect soon after joining the Haverhill Hustlers at 17. Once, just before the start of a game, umpire Steve Mahoney confronted Billy Hamilton with a demand that he get his "mascot" off the field. "Mascot nothing," snapped Hamilton. "That's my shortstop and he is one of the best you've seen." Stuffy undoubtedly had to swallow insults from the veterans, but he bore up well, earning some respect with his hustle on the field, and the way he stood in there at the plate against a level of pitching he had never seen before. Spring of 1909 was before the days of the "Grapefruit League" when big league teams play a predetermined schedule of training camp games with other major league clubs. While there may have been a few outside games that March, Connie Mack liked to keep his men busy with intra-squad contests in which he pitted his veterans, the "Regulars," against the "Yannigans," made up of substitutes, rookies and other hopefuls who were trying to make the team. The latter must have included Stuffy along with the talented Joe Jackson, a raw, unlettered lad who wasn't ready for the big time yet. Later he'd be remembered as "Shoeless" Joe Jackson, a star for the Chicago White Sox and a tragic figure among eight players barred from the game for life by newly appointed Commissioner Kenesaw Mountain Landis following the Black Sox scandal, in which gamblers bribed some of the Chicago men to "throw" the 1919 World Series.

Although Stuffy had a signed contract, there was no guarantee he would make the team. An 18-year-old rookie was unusual in the majors. But Connie Mack was impressed enough to describe his newest recruit as "the best natural ballplayer I ever saw." Stuffy was smart, listened to coaching, and displayed all the baseball instincts Mack looked for. When it came time to break camp and head north to Philadelphia for the start of the American League season, Stuffy McInnis was along for the ride while Joe Jackson was sent to a minor league team for more seasoning. Stuffy's progress that spring was followed, a bit sporadically, by the Beverly press. The *Times*, in its edition of April 13, informed readers in a story headlined "Stuffy Showed Up Well," that "Stuffy McInnis, the old Beverly player who is now with the Philadelphia Athletics, made good in his first game yesterday against the Boston Americans. He was at the bat four times, got a hit, made two putouts, three assists, and was credited (sic) with one error." That April 12 game, in which the A's defeated the Red Sox 8-1, was the first ever played in Philadelphia's new Shibe Park and drew 30,000 fans, more people than young Stuffy had ever seen in one place. His appearance in the opening day lineup should not be taken as an indication that he had earned a starting position. But the A's regular shortstop, Jack Barry from Holy Cross College in Worcester, Mass., was injured that day so Stuffy got to start in his place. That made him the youngest active player in the American League for the '09 season. On May 1, the *Times* quoted from a story in the *Haverhill Gazette* that told how "Stuffy's work has pleased Connie Mack." The story went on to say that Mack planned to keep the kid on the big club's roster at least for one circuit around the American League parks, and "at present there is little doubt that he can stay with the Athletics for the season."

At that time, there was no such thing as a "farm system" for major league ball clubs. A team that wanted to send an extra player out for more seasoning could lend him to a minor league club, or sell that team his contract with a proviso that the big league club could buy it back at the end of the season, or sooner, if needed. It wasn't until the 1930s that Branch Rickey, the front office genius who a decade later with the Brooklyn Dodgers would break the color line by choosing Jackie Robinson to join the Dodgers, started a farm system for the St. Louis Cardinals. Rickey bought outright or worked out agreements with minor league teams at all levels, then signed eager young hopefuls by the dozens to stock them. The idea was to have a steady supply of players coming along to fill openings on the Cardinals, and to use excess rookie talent as trade bait to acquire veteran players from other teams. Soon other clubs started copying Rickey's idea. But in 1909, Connie Mack knew that if he wanted such a talented youngster as Stuffy to learn the game the way the A's field boss wanted him to, the best way was to keep the kid around.

That was how it turned out. Stuffy worked out with, traveled on the trains with, and roomed in hotels with his elders on the Athletics roster throughout the 1909 campaign, and although he could only hope at that point, it cemented his place as a major leaguer for 17 more memorable years. But after his opening day success, he would, like many a rookie before and after him, spend most of his time riding the bench. He appeared in only 19 games, batting .239 with 11 hits in 46 official times at bat, with 4 runs batted in. One of his hits was a home run, one of only 20 he collected in his long career. It was, of course, baseball's "dead ball" era, but Stuffy, who never weighed more than 162 pounds, was built to be a line drive hitter, not a long ball slugger. Over the following eight seasons with Philadelphia, he would only once have a batting average below .300, then as now a benchmark for excellence. In the field as a rookie he played mostly shortstop as a fill-in for Barry, and although he was charged with 10 errors in 14 games, Mack didn't lose confidence in his potential. Mostly, Stuffy watched from the bench, absorbed the atmosphere, and learned the ways of a big league ball club. While it must have been hard at times for a teenager accustomed to playing regularly, he used the time well. Avidly, he mastered the intricacies of baseball strategy – the little things that often make the difference between winning and losing a close game -- from talking with and listening to Mack and the veterans on the team such as the much-respected first baseman Harry Davis. Mack urged the lad to study opposing players to look for strengths that had to be respected and weaknesses that could be exploited. He learned the importance of signals, and used his bench time to watch for the other team's signals so closely that he became an expert at stealing signs, an accomplishment his manager noted with satisfaction. Connie Mack wasn't one for cheating, but swiping an opponent's signs was just clever baseball. From watching his elders, Stuffy learned when it was all right for a player to question an umpire's call and when it was best just to walk away.

To give the youngster some needed playing time, Mack at one point during the season "loaned" Stuffy for 10 days or so to a team representing the somewhat tawdry seaside resort town of Atlantic City, N.J. Baseball researchers have never found any evidence that the Atlantic City team in 1909 was part of a formal league; perhaps, like the Beverly team, it booked games with all comers. But the surviving record shows that Stuffy played shortstop in nine games for Atlantic City, collecting 11 hits in 30 at bats for a .367 average. Except for his short stint in Haverhill and one post-retirement position as a player-manager, it would be his only experience in the minor leagues. After that brief chance at some game action, he returned to the Athletics.

In the spring of 1910, Stuffy had earned the status of "veteran" big leaguer even though he was only 19 years old. There was no doubt that

Connie Mack would keep him on the roster, but it was also the case that no starting position was available for him and he had to bide his time once again in a backup role as a versatile utility infielder. At least he doubled his playing time over his rookie season, getting into 38 games, 17 at shortstop, 5 at second base, 4 at third base, and once, when Mack ran short of outfielders, filling in as a member of the "pasture crew." (He had, of course, played a lot of right field as a 16-year-old on the Beverly team.) Stuffy impressed his teammates with his stronger batting skills, going 22 for 73 for a .301 average, with 12 RBI, 2 doubles, and legging out 4 triples. Perhaps more importantly he improved his defensive play, committing only 5 errors in 77 fielding chances. The Athletics won the American League pennant in 1910, but Stuffy never got into a World Series game. At least he was able to soak in the excitement from his seat in the dugout, and he must have had quite a few stories to tell his folks and friends that winter back in Gloucester.

What a change in fortune came over the career of Stuffy McInnis when he rejoined the Athletics in 1911. At 20, and after two seasons as a bench player for a very good team, he must have been eager to step into the regular lineup and show everyone what he could do. After all, Mack had called him a "natural." But where? With Jack Barry on hand, shortstop, Stuffy's primary position, was locked up. Mack had acquired Eddie Collins to play second base and the hard-hitting Frank "Home Run" Baker was the every day man at third. The outfield was set, too. But there was a job opening about to come along, at first base. The immensely popular Harry Davis, an old National Leaguer and native Philadelphian who was fondly known as "Jasper" to the admiring Athletics' fans, had been holding down first base for the Mack-men since the founding of the American League in 1901. Chosen by Connie Mack to be the first captain of the A's, Jasper Davis led the major leagues in home runs four consecutive seasons from 1904-07, and in RBI in '05 and '06. But by 1911 he was closing in on age 38, and his once mighty skills were fast eroding. Not only were his creaky legs hampering him in fielding his position, his batting eye was slipping, too, and he was having trouble getting around on a good fastball.

Just who first suggested giving Stuffy McInnis a shot at playing first base, where he had never performed before, is somewhat in dispute. Stuffy himself, in later years, claimed to have volunteered, once telling an interviewer that "I got tired of seeing six-foot tall first basemen fail to make the catch. So I decided to become a first baseman myself." According to a story published in the *Cleveland Plain Dealer* in the fall of

1911, probably at the time Harry Davis was hired to manage the Indians for the 1912 season, the idea came from Davis himself. Like most managers, Connie Mack favored tall men at first base. They were better targets, plus they could jump higher and stretch further for high, wide or low throws. Although "official" baseball statistics list Stuffy's height at 5 foot 9, other accounts including a hometown story at the time of his death insist he was only 5'8. The story is that once Davis realized he couldn't last out the 1911 season as an everyday player, he had a conversation with Connie Mack that went something like this:

> Davis: "Why don't you give McInnis a try at first base?"
>
> Mack: "He's too small."
>
> Davis: "He will get any high throws that any first baseman would get. Besides, our infielders will not make many high throws."

Author Norman Lee Macht, in his book "Connie Mack and the Early Years of Baseball," wrote this (p. 502): "Just how or even whose idea it was to make a first baseman out of Stuffy McInnis depends on what you read. For two years, Mack had been studying where to play the Gloucester lad, now twenty and still, Mack maintained, the greatest natural player he had yet seen. The only looming opening in the Athletics lineup was at first base."

With the decline in dependable old Harry Davis's skills becoming obvious, it appears that Mack let Stuffy work out some at first base during spring training, despite harassment from another taller, unsuccessful first base candidate, who tried to push the youngster aside. But any expectation that McInnis might start the 1911 season as the A's regular first baseman would have to wait. Jack Barry badly sprained an ankle, so Stuffy had to fill in for him at shortstop while Davis hung in there as the first baseman. But with Barry healthy again and Jasper slumping mightily, the switch was made in May. So was born the foursome that forever has been remembered as "Connie Mack's $100,000 infield" (a fortune in those days) – Frank Baker at third, Barry at short, the incomparable Eddie Collins at second and McInnis at first. With the pitching of Eddie Plank (whose brother Ira had pitched a game for Beverly in 1907), the Chippewa Indian Albert "Chief" Bender, and Herb Pennock, with an outfield anchored by such stalwarts as Rube Oldring and Danny Murphy, and massive catcher Ira Thomas, the Athletics of 1911 were a formidable outfit.

Stuffy's debut at first base came not without an anxious moment or two for Connie Mack, although not in a ball game. The manager was a strong believer in crisp infield defense, and now he had the people he wanted at every position. In Mack's view, how you practiced was how you played. But now, as he watched his team work out before a game, he was startled to see his infielders make an occasional bad throw to first. The idea was Stuffy's. He realized that if he was to master his new position, he had to learn to deal with the poor throws that were inevitable, especially when an infielder had to throw off balance or in a hurry to make a play. So he asked Baker, Barry and Collins to deliberately give him the occasional low, wide or high throw in practice so he could learn how to handle it. "We had fun," the late Hall of Famer Eddie Collins remembered in later years. "We never worked, we only played. Stuffy used to yell at us during practice, telling us not to make the throws so good. Make'em bad and give him some practice." Once Mack was made aware of what was going on, he gave Stuffy credit for his initiative and stopped worrying that his infielders were becoming careless and sloppy. And Stuffy, happy that he at last had a regular spot in the lineup, was perfecting the skills that were to make him one of the best, if not the best, defensive first basemen in the history of the game. What makes his achievement all the more remarkable is that unlike today's first basemen with their "claw" gloves, photographs show that Stuffy's mitt was a little round thing barely bigger than a ping-pong paddle. With it he compiled a lifetime fielding average of .993, handling 21,360 fielding chances in 1,995 games at first base over 16 seasons, while making only 160 errors. He begrudged every one of those errors.

Stuffy also batted a robust .321 in 1911, with 150 hits, 77 RBI, 13 doubles, 3 home runs and 23 stolen bases. It was one of those home runs that would go down in baseball lore as the most unusual inside-the-park round tripper ever. It's a baseball axiom that the one base you cannot steal is first. You have to earn your way there through a base hit, by drawing a walk, being hit by a pitch, or hitting the ball and taking advantage of a defensive lapse by the opposition. On that memorable day, Stuffy cleverly took advantage of a new rule to steal not only first base, but second, third and home as well. He did it against the Boston Red Sox on June 27, 1911, in a game at the Huntington Avenue Grounds, now part of the Northeastern University campus. It was the last season the Sox played there, before opening Fenway Park in 1912.

Ban Johnson, the founder and president of the American League, had become exercised over what he considered to be the increasingly slow pace of the game. Ban believed that no nine-inning ball game ever should take more than two hours to play, but now the official game reports crossing his desk indicated that the two-hour line was being broken too often. One contest had taken a scandalous 2 hours and 40 minutes. (Can you imagine what Ban Johnson would think of today's 210 minute major league marathons, with three minutes between every half inning to allow for five or six TV and radio commercial messages?) The league president searched his mind for ways to speed up the game. One thing that he thought was unnecessary was the pitcher warmups between innings. Pitchers were allowed up to five practice pitches to loosen up their arm, and most used them all. So Johnson issued at edict to umpires and managers. He didn't specifically "ban" all warmup pitches, but he ordered his umpires to resume play the instant the leadoff batter was ready to step into the box. If it reduced the time between half innings, that was what was wanted.

While Connie Mack eschewed cheating, he wanted his players to take advantage of any opportunity that presented itself. Stuffy had decided, without making his intention known, to give Ban Johnson's new rule a test, and he waited for the right opportunity. It came after the seventh inning that June day, with the A's leading the Red Sox, 6-3, and Stuffy due to bat first in the top of the eighth. The instant the Red Sox made their last out, Stuffy ran to the dugout, grabbed his bat and dashed toward home plate. The Boston fielders, discouraged to be losing in the late innings, were jogging a bit wearily toward their positions. Boston pitcher Ed Karger picked up the baseball; catcher Les Nunamaker strapped on his mask and moved behind the plate. Just as Karger went into his motion to throw his first warmup pitch, Stuffy, who must have winked at plate umpire John Egan to let him know mischief was intended, jumped into the batter's box and swung at the rather soft throw, driving the ball into the outfield between Tris Speaker and Duffy Lewis, whose backs were still to the infield. Thinking that it must be an errant ball, they paid no attention as McInnis dropped his bat, raced to first base and turned toward second. By the time the astonished Boston infielders could warn their outfielders to track down the baseball, Stuffy was approaching third base. He rounded it, tore for home, stepped on the plate and looked to Egan. The umpire, thinking of Ban Johnson, gave the home run signal as Stuffy's teammates shouted with glee and Mack smiled at his young protégé's clever trick.

The Red Sox, of course, had a different view of things. Out of the dugout stormed manager Patsy Donovan to confront Egan. How could it be a legal pitch when his fielders weren't even in position, and when nobody had heard the umpire call Play? Besides, Donovan claimed that one of the Athletics was still on the playing field when Stuffy took his cut. Egan might have sensed that Patsy's argument was just, but any umpire who let himself be talked into reversing a decision never would hear the end of it from players and managers thereafter. Besides, there was Ban Johnson's order, which Egan wasn't about to flout. Donovan bellowed to the umpires, the writers in the press box and the grumbling fans, who now realized what they had just seen, that he was playing the game under protest. That meant he and Egan had to sign an official letter stating the facts as they saw them. When the protest reached the president's office, Ban must have wanted to go out for a drink. If he ruled in favor of the Red Sox he would be ridiculed for overturning his own edict. When he calmed down, he must have considered that Stuffy had picked the right moment. The incident had no impact on the outcome of the ball game, save for adding a run to the final score of the A's victory margin. Protest denied. So the home run stands forever in the record book, the weirdest of the 20 Stuffy hit over his long career. But realizing that he had created a monster that had the potential to make a travesty of the game, Ban Johnson revoked his "hurry up" order in favor of a general admonition to keep the game moving.

The Athletics captured the American League pennant for the second year in a row, and would face John McGraw's New York Giants in the 1911 World Series. Stuffy McInnis, who'd had to watch the 1910 classic from the bench, must have looked forward eagerly to the Series now that he had proved himself as one of Mack's regulars for a full season. But the record shows that it was Harry Davis, not Stuffy, who played first base for the A's throughout their six-game triumph over the Giants. At first glance someone might think that Connie Mack succumbed to sentiment and decided to give his old friend one last World Series triumph as a player. But that wasn't the case, as Mack had no choice other than to summon old Jasper from his seat in the dugout. Stuffy didn't play only because he couldn't play. On Sept. 25, in the dying days of the regular season, the young first baseman was hit on the right wrist by a pitched ball thrown by George Mullin of the Detroit Tigers, causing him to double over in pain. The team doctor determined that no bones were broken, but Stuffy's wrist and forearm swelled up so badly that he could neither grip a bat nor throw a baseball. While it was hoped that the swelling would go down in time for the World Series, that wasn't the case. Jasper Davis drew his old bones together and acquitted himself well, to the delight of the fans who still loved him. In the final inning of game 6, with the Athletics about to wrap up the championship, Connie sent Stuffy into the game at first base so he could at least say he had played in the World Series. He had the honor of recording the final putout, but the disappointment must have stayed with him all winter. Frank Baker earned his immortal nickname in that series by winning two games with home run clouts.

With Mack's approval, Harry Davis accepted an offer to manage the Cleveland Indians for the 1912 season. He tried to bring some of the A's-style discipline to the woebegone Indians, but his players failed to respond. In mid-August, with Cleveland mired in sixth place and going nowhere, Jasper resigned in disgust. He'd return to Philadelphia as a coach in 1913 and for several years thereafter. His pal Mack always found a way to insert the beloved Jasper into a game so he would have another line in the record book, right up through 1917. So popular was he in Philadelphia that his friends talked him into entering politics. He ran for a seat on the city's Common Council and was elected, making him Councilman Davis. He lived in Philly until his death in 1947. Davis's biography in "The Ballplayers" includes this: "As a coach he instructed Stuffy McInnis, who became one of the game's best first basemen and played on four of Mack's pennant winners."

In 1912, Stuffy, now a hardened veteran of 21 and fully healed from his injury, reported to the Athletics determined to make up for the disappointing end to his previous season. Mack even seems to have used him as a base coach while the A's were at bat. He posted what actually were his most impressive individual statistics, batting a career high (as a regular player) .327, with 186 hits and a career high 101 RBI, while playing all but one of the team's 154 games. *Harvard Crimson* writer Stephen N. Cady, quoted in February of 1949 from "a yellowing newspaper clipping dated Aug. 5, 1912" which had this to say about young Mr. McInnis:

"It's worth the price of admission to see McInnis play. A little over five feet eight inches in height and carrying about 150 pounds, Stuffy is the whole works around one of the greatest infields ever gotten together. He wears a uniform that has been through many a battle and his glove appears to the onlooker to be bigger than himself. He is always working. While his teammates are going to the bat he scampers around the coaching lines begging them to connect with the ball. When his time arrives he rushes to the bench, picks up a bat and without any ceremony, walks right up to the ball. He has a fancy way of meeting it – chopping it right on the nose and whenever he connects, you can depend on seeing it take the long route." That last statement is of course an exaggeration, since Stuffy never was known as a long ball slugger. Stuffy himself mused on the frustrations involved in trying to smash a long one against the pitchers he faced back then: "It was almost impossible to hit a ball out of the park in those days. Everything favored the pitchers. The ball was deader than it is today, and the pitchers all chewed tobacco, so that by the eighth or ninth inning the ball was like a chunk of coal."

But despite all their talent, the A's lost the 1912 pennant to the Boston Red Sox, who were led by their incomparable center fielder Tris Speaker, and ace pitcher "Smoky" Joe Wood, who won 34 games that year while losing only 5. While taking nothing away from the Red Sox, Connie Mack made it clear how disappointed he was when his favored Athletics failed to capture a third straight American League pennant. "If ever a club suffered from overconfidence, it was my 1912 team," said Mack. In 1913, the A's held spring training in San Antonio, Texas, the place where Texans began their struggle to throw off the yoke of Mexican rule, with the goal of regaining the pinnacle of the American League. While Mack may not have talked to his men about "remembering the Alamo," the Athletics' boss made it clear from the beginning that he had not forgotten the team's letdown of the previous year. According to the Philadelphia Athletics Historical Society: "A new psychology permeated the camp as Mack worked his players harder than in the past and reminded them incessantly that lackadaisical play and smug attitudes had cost the A's the pennant the previous year." It can be expected that his 22-year-old first baseman welcomed the tough approach. Stuffy hadn't forgotten how the wrist injury cost him his chance to play in the 1911 World Series, and he was eager for another shot at the extra paycheck. The $100,000 Infield was now the toast of baseball, with the figure referring not to the salaries of the players (who in total earned far less than that), but to the prevailing opinion that the combined talents of the fabulous four were "beyond value." Unlike today, when multi-million dollar signings make headlines, player contracts in the early 20th century attracted little attention. While an occasional contract of the time might have drawn some interest in the press, that was never the case with Stuffy. His official record in "The Baseball Almanac" lists his salary for every year from 1909 to 1927 as "undetermined." What Stuffy earned in 1913 and every other year in which he played was strictly between him and the ball club. Mack's talented team did succeed in finishing first again, with Stuffy continuing to sting the ball at a .324 clip and starring at first base. Roaring out of their training camp with a new determination, the Athletics were in first place by the end of April and never relinquished the lead. They won by 6½ games over the Washington Senators, despite the magnificent pitching of Washington's young Walter Johnson, who won 36 games while losing only 7. "Chief" Bender picked up 21 wins and Eddie Plank 18, with Mack successfully employing the somewhat risky strategy of calling both of his ace pitchers into the game as late inning relievers to "close" for his younger hurlers. "Home Run" Baker led the league both in four-baggers (12) and runs batted in (117). This time Stuffy finally got to play every game in the World Series, again against John McGraw's New York Giants, but another personal disappointment was in store. His batting eye deserted him, and he could manage just 2 hits in 17 at bats for a pathetic .118 average and 2 RBI. Despite McInnis's weak hitting, the Philadelphians came out on top in the World Series. 4 games to 1, as Bender pitched two wins, Plank one, and young Joe Bush was the winning pitcher in the third game.

While the 1914 team might have been the best of the early Connie Mack era, it in fact drew down the curtain on that era and brought about the breakup of a great ball club. Stuffy's batting average "slipped" to .314, a mark many big leaguers would envy, but he also compiled an astonishing .995 fielding average, making only 7 errors in 1,515 chances. The Athletics went into the 1914 World Series heavily favored over the Boston Braves, a team that unaccountably had come from last place on the Fourth of July to win the National League flag. To the astonishment of the baseball world, the lowly Braves demolished the Mack-men by taking the Series in four straight games. Stuffy again struggled at bat, going 2 for 14 for a .143 average.

Connie Mack had big problems as the '14 season ended. First was the attitude of the Philadelphia fans, some of whom were so disgusted at the World Series collapse that they threatened to stay home in 1915. An even worse threat came from the Federal League. Organized as a minor circuit in 1913, the Feds decided the next year to award themselves major league status. Now for 1915 they went all out to raid the two established major leagues by offering lucrative contracts to induce players to jump. Federal League team owners hoped to sign a nucleus of three or four highly paid big name stars to draw fans, and fill in around them with lesser lights from the fringes of the majors and the minor leagues. The A's, who always struggled to make ends meet financially, would be a prime target. Mack wasn't about to see his players go for no return, so he broke up the club. He traded Jack Barry to the Red Sox and sold Eddie Collins to the Chicago White Sox. (He'd be one of the honest players whom the gamblers didn't dare to approach when they "fixed" the 1919 World Series in baseball's darkest episode.) Home Run Baker was so disgusted that he opted to sit out the entire 1915 season in protest. Of the $100,000 Infield, only Stuffy McInnis, loyal to his mentor Connie Mack, was left with the A's in 1915. The Federal League folded its tents after that year, but the damage was done. Philadelphia dropped from first place to the league basement in 1915, and finished last again over the following two seasons. Stuffy still batted over .300 except in 1916, when he just missed out at .295. But after the 1917 debacle, when the Athletics lost 107 of their 154 games, Mack realized he would have to let Stuffy go as well. After the third last place finish and loss of ticket sales, the A's coffers were nearly empty. Mack asked McInnis to take a pay cut for 1918, but Stuffy, at the height of his career at 27 and boasting nine years of big league experience, refused. A trade was the only solution. At least Mack sent his star first baseman "home" to Boston. In January of 1918 it was announced that Stuffy McInnis had been traded to the Red Sox for three players – first baseman Larry Gardner, outfielder Tilly Walker, and catcher Forrest "Hick" Cady. The prodigal son could take his talents to Fenway Park, where his friends from the North Shore could see him play more than the few times a year when Philadelphia came to town.

BOSTON, ELSIE, MANCHESTER, 1918, THE BABE, AND A BEVERLY CAMEO

"Jack McInnis is a cool, cautious citizen in a pinch of this kind"
  – New York Times, Sept. 12, 1918

Coming home to Boston in 1918 set Stuffy McInnis up to take part in one of the strangest seasons in the history of major league baseball, one that ended in the Red Sox last World Series championship for 86 years, until the 2004 ball club finally broke what came to be known as the "Curse of the Bambino." It was the year George Herman "Babe" Ruth both pitched the Sox to victory over the Chicago Cubs and showed the hitting power that soon converted him from a feared left handed pitcher to an even more feared slugger who played the outfield every day. It was a World Series that came close to never being played at all, and which ended with the players on both teams in near revolt over their measly financial shares. The year of 1918 also saw the terrible influenza pandemic that claimed many lives in the United States and throughout the world at a time when antibiotic drugs were unknown and the flu often led to fatal cases of pneumonia. It also was a time of war, now called World War I. The United States had entered the war against Germany and its allies in the spring of 1917, after three years of bitter stalemate had depleted the resources and manpower of Britain and France. Troopships were carrying American volunteers and draftees across the Atlantic to join the bitter fighting in the trenches

28

of France. Factories were humming around the clock to churn out war materiel.

The 1918 Red Sox were coming off a 1917 season that saw them win the World Series in five games over the Brooklyn Dodgers, their second straight world championship while Stuffy and the A's were bringing up the AL rear. The Sox had played their "home" games in the '17 series down Commonwealth Avenue at Braves Field, which with its 40,000 capacity could hold more fans than Fenway Park. Ruth won 24 games that season and batted a lusty .325, something no pitcher was supposed to do. Born in 1895, the son of a Baltimore saloonkeeper, Ruth grew up running wild in the streets. Sent as a boy to St. Mary's Home, a Roman Catholic Church-run industrial residential school for orphans and delinquents, for his own salvation, his raw athletic skills soon caught the attention of the religious Brother who directed the baseball program. He was quickly promoted to the "varsity" team that featured much older boys. When Ruth was old enough to leave what was essentially a reform school-orphanage, Brother Gilbert arranged for him to be signed by Jack Dunn, who ran the old Baltimore Orioles of the high minor International League. Dunn polished Ruth's pitching technique, and in 1914, when the Babe was 19, he sold the promising lefty's contract to the Red Sox.

The Red Sox in 1918 had new ownership. Joseph J. Lannin, with two championships under his belt, decided to retire while he was on top. On December 4, 1917, the Boston newspapers reported that Lannin had sold the ball club and the ballpark to two New York "theatrical men," Harry Frazee and Hugh J. Ward. While the purchase price was reported to be in excess of $1,000,000, Frazee seems to have raised much of the money on promissory notes. Frazee, a native of Peoria, Illinois who owned theaters in New York and Chicago, was best known as a show producer whose goal in life was to produce a Broadway blockbuster. Professional baseball would be a secondary outlet. Meeting with the Boston press in mid-December, Frazee and Ward, made what Frederick G. Lieb, author of a 1947 book "The Boston Red Sox," wrote what was "a favorable impression on the town's sports scribes." Bill Carrigan had retired as manager at the end of 1917, so Frazee offered the managerial job to second baseman Jack Barry, Stuffy's old pal from the $100,000 Infield, who had been dealt to Boston by Connie Mack before the 1915 season. A photo in Lieb's book from the winter of 1918, attributed to *The Sporting News*, shows Babe Ruth and Stuffy McInnis, both wearing overcoats to show they had just come in from the cold, preparing to sign their 1918 contracts in the Red Sox executive suite, with Frazee and Ed Barrow seated, holding the paperwork. Hugh Ward soon sailed away to Australia, leaving Frazee in charge of the ball club. Barry, the old Holy Cross star, had a question for Frazee before accepting the offer to manage. Would his decisions be controlled and second-guessed by the ownership, or would he be allowed to be a real manager, as Carrigan had been. Frazee's reply: "Absolutely, Jack. Whatever you say goes."

The return to Massachusetts also provided Stuffy with another opportunity – to change from a bachelor who had lived out of hotels during nine long baseball seasons in Philadelphia to a married man with a home situated between the towns of his birth and his "discovery." For Stuffy, the love of his life was Elsie Dow of Manchester, the pretty seaside town located between Gloucester and Beverly. Just how Stuffy and Elsie first met seems to be one of those details that has been lost to the modern researcher. Stuffy's grandson, Richard Littlefield, son of Eileen, the McInnis's only child, and her husband Charles Littlefield, says that his mother, who lived until March of 2009, never mentioned to him anything about her parents' courtship. Eileen's best friend since childhood, Mary Mahoney of Beverly, similarly has no recollection of being told that story. It is safe to conclude that the ballplayer and his future bride, living within a few miles of each other, had become close long before they decided to tie the knot. Now with Stuffy traded to the Red Sox, they could do so. The attractive house at 11 Tappan Street in Manchester, an easy walk off Beach Street from the town center, in which the couple lived for the rest of their lives, was built for them. Elsie Dow was a Manchester native. She was born there on April 6, 1891, making her about six months younger than her husband, the daughter of Charles and Margaret (Clougherty) Dow. Her father was a well-known local businessman who owned the Manchester Fish Market on Summer Street for many years before his passing in 1940. The Dow family home was nearby, at 25 Summer St. A 1915 directory lists Elsie as being single. Obviously she was waiting for her ballplayer to attain a more settled position; now, at age 27 and going to play in Boston, they could be married.

As the Red Sox reported for spring workouts in March of 1918, the club was decidedly in a state of flux, thanks to the demands of World War I, then called the Great War. Several players already had traded baseball flannels for military uniforms, and others soon joined them. And it was Ed Barrow, not Barry, who ran the show from the dugout. Barry had joined the U.S. Navy during the winter, so Frazee asked Barrow, the former president of the International League and future president of the

New York Yankees, to step in as field boss. Among the Sox stars who enlisted in the Navy to avoid becoming infantry fodder were left fielder Duffy Lewis, pitcher Herb Pennock, Del Gainor, Mike McNally, Jimmy Walsh, and third baseman Fred Thomas. Ernie Shore, another top pitcher, was awarded a commission as ensign in the Navy. Dutch Leonard, after starting the season with the team, also joined his mates who were wearing the Navy uniform. That left a lot of holes to fill. But according to Frederick G. Lieb, Frazee initiated some smart deals, acquiring center fielder Amos Strunk, catcher Wally Schang, and pitcher Joe Bush. To replace the absent Barry at second base, the Sox swung a trade with Cincinnati to acquire another local guy, Dave Shean from Arlington, Mass. and Fordham University. Shean had another local connection, as at one time while in college a decade before he had played for Dick Madden's old Beverly team. Old-timer George Whiteman was picked up from the minors to fill in for Lewis in left. As for Stuffy, Barrow had one of the game's best first basemen on his roster, but he couldn't use him there, at least not for a while. He still had Dick Hoblitzel back to play first, but with Thomas absent there was no qualified third baseman in sight. So Barrow asked McInnis to open the season at the "hot corner," a position Stuffy had played only four times as a fill-in for the Athletics back in 1910. He certainly acquitted himself well in the unfamiliar position. In 23 games at third, he handled 77 fielding chances while making only one error, and initiated eight double plays. But less than a month into the season Hoblitzel was gone, too, accepting an officer's commission in the Army. That meant Stuffy was returned to his familiar spot at first, and the search for a new third baseman began as various people were tried. Said shortstop Everett Scott: "Everybody plays third base for the Red Sox. Just as soon as I know the name of the guy who's playing alongside of me, somebody else turns up to play the bag."

One thing the war, and the Sox resulting lack of offensive punch, did achieve was making an outfielder out of Babe Ruth. The Babe was still one of the aces of the Boston pitching staff in 1918, but his prowess with the bat could not be ignored. With Whiteman struggling at the plate, Barrow decided that on any day when Ruth wasn't pitching and the opposition was using a right-handed pitcher, he would insert the Babe into the lineup in left field. Whiteman played only against southpaws. It turned out to be a spectacularly successful move. Playing a total of 95 games in a shortened season, Ruth batted .300 with 95 hits, including 26 doubles, 11 triples and 11 home runs, tying for the American League lead in round-trippers in what was still a "dead ball" era. That was a huge boost for a team that could manage only a collective .249 batting average. Stuffy, who as a newlywed of 27 seemed to have been in no danger from the draft, had his worst career batting average, .272. Nevertheless, he contributed 56 RBI, 11 doubles, 5 triples and 32 sacrifice hits. He was his usual sturdy self on defense, posting a .992 fielding average after returning to first base, with just 9 errors in 1,146 chances.

The Red Sox took over first place on July 6, and never surrendered the lead again. But the World Series of 1918, so long the subject of a derisive chant by New York Yankees' fans who loved to rub it in to the Red Sox until Boston finally broke the "jinx" in 2004, almost never got played. While major league baseball had been allowed to continue despite the war, the conflict caught up with the game in 1918. Newton D. Baker, Secretary of War in the Cabinet of President Woodrow Wilson, hit the major leagues with an order that the playing season must come to an end by Labor Day, Sept. 2, or all of its personnel would be subject to the "Work or Fight" order. That was designed to force able bodied, non-drafted young men to either join the military or take full-time jobs in a defense industry. With team owners standing to lose all of their September ticket sales and concession revenue, they were in no mood to end the season by the third week in August to allow two teams to play a World Series. It looked as though no world champion would be crowned and no extra paychecks for members of the National and American League champions in the curtailed season. But all hope was not lost. In the years before 1920 when baseball got its first commissioner, Kenesaw Mountain Landis, in the wake of the Black Sox scandal, the game was ruled by a National Commission, consisting of the presidents of the two major leagues and a chairman agreed upon by both leagues. Garry Hermann, the Commission chairman, fired off a letter to Baker on Aug. 11, asking him to suspend the order long enough for the two league champions to compete after the holiday. Baseball, Hermann argued, was important to the morale of the nation and having a World Series would boost that morale, plus the sport would contribute a share of the proceeds to war charities. An answer came back from General Enoch Crowder, the national draft director. Writing on behalf of Baker, Crowder informed Hermann that his request for an extension was approved, provided the Series was completed no later than Sept. 16. The Red Sox and the Chicago Cubs, who led the National League when the dreaded Labor Day rolled around, got to decide the championship after all. But it was perhaps the most contentious World Series ever played, while thankfully lacking the sordid, crooked drama of the Series the following year.

Because of the distance between the cities and the wartime travel restrictions, baseball's National Commission ordered that the first three games were to be played in Chicago, after which the teams would entrain for Boston to finish things out, anywhere from one to four games. Having the first three games at home gave the Cubs an obvious advantage. With smaller crowds expected due to wartime work schedules and fear of influenza, the Sox used Fenway Park instead of the larger Braves Field. The Cubs, however, chose to play in the bigger Comiskey Park on the South Side of town, home of the White Sox. Four of baseball's most experienced umpires were assigned to work the series – George Hildebrand and Brick Owens of the American League, Bill Klem and Hank O'Day of the "senior circuit."

Knowing the importance of grabbing at least one win on the road, Barrow chose Babe Ruth as his pitcher for the opening contest, played on September 5 before a disappointingly small crowd of 19,274 while Cubs field boss Fred Mitchell went with "Hippo" Vaughn. The Babe came through in a big way, pitching shutout ball as the visitors blanked the Cubs, 1-0. Another player who came through in the clutch was Stuffy McInnis. After being forced to watch the 1911 series from the bench with his injury, and then performing miserably at the plate when the Athletics played for the championship in 1913 and 1914, Mr. McInnis was eager to redeem himself. His chance came in the top of the fourth inning, when his base hit drove home Dave Shean for the only run of the game. With that win under their belts, the Sox were safe from any threat of being swept in Chicago. The U.S. Navy gave the Sox a boost by granting a furlough to Fred Thomas, the 1917 third baseman, so he could join the team and bolster what had been Boston's weakest position. The Cubs evened things up the next day with a 3-1 win, in a game that saw tempers flare and a couple of near brawls, but the Sox responded by taking the third game on September 7, 2-1, behind the pitching of Carl Mays. Stuffy scored the winning run in the fourth, an inning that saw consecutive hits by McInnis, Schang and Everett Scott. Fred Whiteman, playing left field instead of Ruth, saved the day when he robbed Dode Paskert of a possible home run with a sensational catch. Said Reach's "Guide:" "Ruth could not have made the catch Whiteman did, one of the best in the Series." So the Red Sox were in a happy mood as they boarded the train for Boston, with Monday, Sept. 8, being an off day for travel, holding a lead in the series. Both teams rode the special train, called the "National Commission Special." Back home at Fenway on the 9th, a less than capacity crowd of 22,183 saw the home team extend its series lead to 3-1 by outlasting the Cubs, 3-2. Boston jumped out to a 2-0 lead on a triple by Ruth that drove home Stuffy and Whiteman, only to see the Cubs tie the score in the top of the eighth, ending Babe Ruth's record of 29 consecutive scoreless World Series innings pitched. But the Sox regained control in their half of the inning after Mitchell called on "Shufflin' Phil" Douglas, a spitball expert (legal then), to take the mound in relief. Schang singled, took second when one of Douglas's "wet ones" skipped by the catcher for a passed ball, and scored when Douglas fielded Harry Hooper's sacrifice bunt and made a wild throw. The Sox held off the Cubs in the ninth and were now one win away from a third consecutive title in the war-shortened season. The reporter who covered the World Series for *The New York Times* was certainly an admirer of the Red Sox first baseman. Writing on game four for the Sept. 10 edition, the *Times* man told his readers: "The ninth inning saw the wise head of little Jack McInnis play an important part in the timely halt of another Cub rally. No player in the whole series has shown the baseball sense that the first baseman of the Red Sox has displayed." When Connie Mack called the teenage Stuffy "the best natural ballplayer I ever saw" back in 1909, he knew what he was talking about.

Game 5, however, almost didn't happen. If players had been happy earlier, members of both teams were downright surly on Sept. 10, angry enough that they got together and refused to take the field. Fans in the crowd of 24,000 who arrived to see the pre-game warmups were stunned to be confronted by an empty ballfield. It was all about money. Up until 1918, those competing in the World Series took home all of the players' share, based only on the first four games, for obvious reasons. But that year, the National Commission decreed that members of the teams finishing second, third and fourth (the "first division") in each league also must be paid a cut of the Series money. They picked a bad year to do this, with the war cutting drastically into the gate receipts. Red Sox players had earned more than $3,000 in 1917, but this year's winning share figured to be a third of that or less, especially with 10 per cent promised to war charities. They were professionals, and as far as they were concerned they now were playing for nothing. So when the 2 o'clock game time neared, both teams stayed in the clubhouse. Harry Hooper and Les Mann were elected representatives to negotiate for their respective teams. The two members of the National Commission present at the time rejected a demand that the other first division teams be cut out of the series shares, and also turned down a counter proposal that players on the winning side be guaranteed $1,500, with $1,000 to the losers. At that point, according to Lieb, a disgusted Hooper suggested that all of the proceeds, including the owners' share, be donated to the Red Cross. American League President Ban Johnson, the third commission member, had spent the pre-game hours drinking with friends in the bar of the Copley Plaza Hotel. Now he came roaring onto the scene, appealed to Hooper's better nature for the good of the game, and implored, "Harry, go out there and play. The crowd is waiting for you." Hooper and Mann returned to their locker rooms, and after 10 minutes of heated talk the players ran out onto the field. The game was something of an anti-climax as Vaughn got some revenge by shutting out Sad Sam Jones and the Sox, 3-0. But that only delayed Boston's triumph by a day as Mays pitched another 2-1 win, allowing the Cubs just three hits, while Mr. McInnis contributed another clutch hit to drive in Dave Shean with the winning run. Telling of that hit, again, *The New York Times* writer gushed: "Next came to the bat Stuffy McInnis, the modest little graduate of the baseball university of Connie Mack. Jack McInnis is a cool, cautious citizen in a pinch of this kind. If Manager Barrow had his choice, he could not have chosen a better man than this same sawed-off lad from Gloucester," Only 15,238 spectators paid their way into Fenway to see the finale of the 1918 World Series, their team's last world title for 86 years. The *Times* man summed it up on Sept. 12: "Boston is the luckiest spot on earth, for it has never lost a world's series." If only he knew how that comment was jinxing Beantown.

In a self-published book called "The Original Curse," Sean Devaney, a reporter for *The Sporting News*, wrote that one reason for Stuffy's uncharacteristic .272 batting average in 1918 was that he was suffering from boils, which affected his grip. As for the World Series, Devaney said that "McInnis made a sterling play that helped win Game 1 for the Red Sox." Third baseman Fred Thomas, on leave from the Navy, made a hurried, wide throw on a bunt by Charlie Hollacher of the Cubs. Stuffy risked injury by reaching around Hollacher to catch the ball and make the putout. Hugh Fullerton, the legendary baseball reporter who first became suspicious that the 1919 series was not on the up-and-up, described Stuffy's game-saving play: "Two out of three first basemen would have let that ball go and chased it to the stands."

It was certainly a series for pitchers, not hitters, as the winning club managed a meager .186 team batting average with just 9 runs scored, and the Cubs were just a tad better at .210. Not one home run was hit during the six games. As the players had feared, the winners' share came to only $1,108 per man, and the Cubs had to settle for a paltry $671 – chicken feed even in those days. Of course the servicemen who were far from home fighting the war might have considered that an enviable payday. Stuffy's statistical sheet shows he had 5 hits in 20 official at bats, for a .250 average, not great, but a huge improvement over his achievements in the two World Series he took part in while with the Athletics, not counting his token appearance in the 1911 classic. More importantly, some of those hits had come in clutch situations. At least he would have something pleasant to talk about with folks he met over the winter in his new hometown of Manchester.

The 1919 baseball season was a letdown for the Red Sox and their fans, who had become used to winning. Peace had returned after the November 11 Armistice brought an end to the war, and costly reparations soon were to be imposed on Germany by the victorious Allies. Most of our soldiers and sailors, including the ballplayers, had either returned home or were on their way. When the returnees were put together with the players Frazee had acquired in 1918, the Sox now seemingly had a glut of talent and could make some trades. Among those who departed were Ernie Shore, Dutch Leonard and Duffy Lewis, moved to the New York Yankees in a deal that presaged the disaster to come. The Sox fell all the way to sixth place in 1919, the only real bright spot being Babe Ruth. Now assigned to play the outfield on a full-time basis, the Bambino responded by clouting 29 home runs, a remarkable achievement in that era. Stuffy McInnis had a very respectable season, too. Playing in 120 games, he raised his batting average from the .272 of the year before to .305, more in keeping with his lifetime hitting performance. He continued his stellar defensive play at first base, committing only 7 errors for a gaudy fielding average of .995. The American League pennant fell to the talented Chicago White Sox, who were favored over the Cincinnati Reds in the World Series, changed for that year to best 5 out of 9 games. Followers of the game were stunned when the Reds won the title, 5 to 3, over what appeared to be a listless Chicago bunch. It became even more stunning, and baseball's greatest black eye, when news broke that a consortium of gamblers had bribed seven members of the White Sox to "throw" the series. The players, disgusted by the parsimony of owner Charles Comiskey, had been willing to listen when the crooked deal was proposed to them. Public dismay prompted baseball owners to dissolve the National Commission in 1920 and appoint a federal judge, Kenesaw Mountain Landis, to a powerful position as Commissioner of Baseball. Although the "Black Sox" players all were acquitted of criminal charges when their grand jury testimony mysteriously disappeared from the files, their celebration was cut short when Landis banned all eight from the game for life, including Buck Weaver, who had taken no bribe and played the games honestly, but who knew what was afoot and kept quiet. The judge was determined that public trust in professional baseball had to be restored if the game was to survive. New heroes would come along in the 1920s to help make that happen, especially Babe Ruth.

Throughout his long baseball career, Ruth was known as a man who never took training seriously and was a noted carouser off the field. At one point while he was with the Yankees, outfielder "Ping" Bodie was assigned to room with Ruth in the team hotel when the Yanks were on the road. Asked later to describe the experience of rooming with the Bambino, Bodie replied, "I never roomed with Ruth. I roomed with his suitcase." Although we have seen no written evidence, tradition has it that the Red Sox, knowing of Ruth's lifestyle, assigned the clean living Stuffy McInnis to room with him on road trips in the hope he could keep the big fellow in line. Doubtless Stuffy had little chance to spend much time with the happy-go-lucky Babe. There's another story involving Ruth and Stuffy. Back in 1916, while McInnis was still with the Athletics, he walked into a Boston hotel the night after the lowly A's lost to the Babe at Fenway, and as he did so he spotted Ruth sitting in the lobby. Being of a friendly nature, Stuffy walked up to the Baltimorean and complimented him on his pitching that afternoon. Ruth, who was notorious for not remembering anybody's name and so referred to one and all as "Kid," seemingly didn't recognize the greeter as the man who played first base for the opposing team. "Thanks, kid, I'm glad you could come out to the park and see it," was how Stuffy recalled the Babe's reply.

Speaking of the Babe, he was the catalyst for a cameo return by Stuffy McInnis to Beverly, the town in which his talents were discovered. Ruth was never against picking up a few extra dollars in the off-season with a little barnstorming. That fall Ruth, who had purchased a little farm in rural Massachusetts, toured with a pickup team he called the "Red Sox Independents" (copyright infringement being less of a problem in those days). Certainly the Babe, who had become used to World Series checks for the past three seasons, was trying to make up for the lack of the extra money in 1919. On October 10th he brought his show to Beverly. Perhaps the town still had no team to boast of, or more likely by October it had broken up with players returning to college or work commitments.

So the Beverly exhibition featured the "Sox" against a squad from Marblehead. Ruth signed up Shean and Stuffy, who lived next door in Manchester, along with other players whose names have not been recorded. The game was played on what was then called the "high school athletic field," which in 1921 was named Cooney Field. The fence surrounding the playing field was a goodly distance from home plate, but the crowd that turned out was eager to see if Ruth could "park one." His 29 homers for Boston that season had already had made him a legendary slugger. They weren't disappointed, and a new local baseball legend was born.

The *Beverly Times* in its edition of Oct. 11 covered the game in a short story headlined, "Red Sox Win from the Marblehead Team." The story read:

> Over 1,500 baseball fans saw the Red Sox Independents defeat the Marblehead team on the Beverly High School athletic field yesterday afternoon, by a score of 2 to 0.

> Babe Ruth was the principal attraction. 'Babe' made his home run which was looked for by the ball fans, which occurred in the sixth inning. 'Stuffy' McInnis, who is no stranger to Beverly ball fans, did good hitting, and Dave Shean, another of Beverly's favorites who at one time played on 'Dick' Madden's team, put up a good game.

> Leahy, for the Marblehead team, played a good game at centrefield (sic), making three handsome catches. Davies pitched a fine game of ball, striking out 'Babe' Ruth the second time at bat. The Red Sox made its first run in the third inning and its second in the sixth inning" (when Ruth connected).

The fans got to see what they came for, and pitcher Davies achieved a feat he could boast about for the rest of his life. Ironically, although of course nobody suspected it, the Beverly game took place at the same time the "crooked" World Series of 1919 was playing out at ballparks in Chicago and Cincinnati. In 2010, a group of Beverly residents including former city Clerk of Committees Dick Kelley was working to provide a memorial at Cooney to commemorate Ruth's historic blast.

It was an exciting moment in Beverly sports history, and the game gave Stuffy one more chance to appear in a game before the "home" fans who had cheered him and cemented his nickname. But there was a touch of sadness attached to that day for anyone in the crowd, presumably most, who rooted for the Boston Red Sox. Although they didn't know it then, it was the Babe's farewell appearance as their favorite. When they next saw him play, it would be in an enemy uniform.

THE EVIL SHOWMAN FROM PEORIA WRECKS THE RED SOX

"It will be impossible to replace the strength Ruth gave the Sox"

  – Johnny Keenan, leader of Boston's Royal Rooters, January 1920

Babe Ruth was the toast of Boston baseball followers in 1919, the first year of peace after the bitter war, with his 29 home runs, including four "grand slams" with the bases loaded, and his colorful ways. But he had angered Frazee before the season by hiring an agent, then referred to as a "manager," and demanding more money prior to signing his contract. Despite the Ruthian power display, the Red Sox had come a long way down from their success of 1916-18, finishing a dismal sixth in the eight-team league, behind even the St. Louis Browns. Now with 1920 coming on, Harry Frazee needed money for his planned theatrical productions. He'd had a modest success with a show called "My Lady Friends," but there were two or three costly flops as well to drain his bank account. Furthermore, the notes of indebtedness he had

40

given Lannon to purchase the ball club in 1918 were coming due. Perhaps the quickest way to raise cash was to unload some of the high-priced talent that had let him down in 1919. There was a team with plenty of money to spend on players, the New York Yankees, who were owned by beer baron Jacob Ruppert and some business partners. Ruppert was determined the Yankees would be the toast of baseball in the 1920s. He had already grabbed Ernie Shore, Dutch Leonard and favorite left fielder Duffy Lewis from the Red Sox in 1919, along with ace pitcher Carl Mays, who had left the Sox in anger after a game in Chicago. Ruppert knew he had a ready seller in Mr. M. Harrison Frazee, whose New York theater was just around the corner from the Yankees' office suite.

On January 9, 1920, headlines in the Boston newspapers left the Boston fans roaring in shock and rage. At that time, of course, radio was still in its experimental stage and all news came from the competing daily papers. Outraged readers learned that Frazee had just sold the beloved Babe Ruth to the New York Yankees for what was reported to be $60,000, but actually involved six figures. On the same day, Yankees president Ruppert called a press conference to announce: "Gentlemen, we have just bought Babe Ruth from Harry Frazee of the Boston Red Sox." According to Frederick Lieb in his 1947 book 'The Boston Red Sox,' Boston Manager Ed Barrow tried unsuccessfully to talk Frazee out of the move. When he failed, he demanded that it be strictly a cash transaction instead of having it masquerade as a "trade" by shipping a couple of Yankee cast-offs to the Red Sox in return. There was more to it. In addition to buying Ruth, the Yankee ownership loaned Frazee another $300,000, taking a mortgage on Fenway Park as collateral. So the Yanks, who at the time were still tenants of the Giants in the Polo Grounds, now owned Boston's American League ballpark.

If Harry Frazee was less than popular with the Fenway Faithful in 1919, he now had descended into the role of perhaps the most despised man in Beantown. A story in *The New York Times* brought out the reaction of the Royal Rooters, an organization of rabid fans, largely Irish, that had marched to the park behind its own band and sat together in a left field section since the early years of the Pilgrims. The Rooters were organized in 1903 by Boston bartender Michael 'Nuf Ced' McGreevey, and adopted the song "Tessie" as their theme tune. Now *The New York Times* reported that the fan club was up in arms over their favorite being dispatched to New York for a wad of cash. "Boston's Royal Rooters are pretty badly disturbed over Ruth's sale. Johnny Keenan, leader of the

Royal Rooters, had this to say: 'Ruth was ninety percent of our club last summer. It will be impossible to replace the strength Ruth gave the Sox. The Batterer is a wonderful player and the fact that he loves the game and plays with his all to win makes him a tremendous asset to a club. The Red Sox management will have an awful time filling the gap caused by his going.'" Most Boston fans, who had adopted the Babe as their own, with Ruth even acquiring a farm in the outer suburbs as his year-round home, excoriated Frazee as a betrayer of the franchise. The owner tried to defend himself by telling the press, "Ruth's twenty-nine homers were more spectacular than useful; they didn't help the Red Sox get out of sixth place." That hardly mollified anyone, especially when the 1920 season unfolded and Ruth, now strictly an outfielder with a big bat, began to lead the Yankees into a new era. In 1920 he made his previous year look puny when he blasted 54 home runs for the Yankees. It wasn't enough to beat out Tris Speaker's Cleveland Indians for the pennant, but it was the shape of things to come. In the wake of the Black Sox scandal, baseball needed new heroes to restore public confidence in the sport. The "dead ball" era was over, and the home run slugger, epitomized by the Bambino, was now king. The Yankees became dominant, and when Ruppert and company constructed the new Yankee Stadium in 1923, it became known as "The House that Ruth Built." Starting that year they won six American League pennants in the '20s alone, and the Babe set a new standard when he bashed 60 homers in 1927. For the Red Sox, 86 years passed between their 1918 world title and the next one in 2004.

How Stuffy McInnis reacted at the time to the sale of the slugger is not recorded, although it can be expected he was not pleased to see the ball club so weakened. But loyal soldier that he was, he continued to give his best to the Red Sox and their disheartened fans. In 1920 he played in all but six of the team's 154 games, pounding out 166 hits in 559 official at bats, including 21 doubles, 3 triples and even 2 home runs, failing to bat .300 or better for just the second time since 1910 but coming very close at .297. In the field he led all American League first baseman with a stellar .996 average, committing only seven errors in 1,684 chances at handling the baseball. The team did not, as many of its followers feared, drop to the league cellar, finishing fifth with a .471 winning percentage. Despite a weak-hitting lineup, solid pitching by lefty Herb Pennock, Joe Bush, Sam Jones and the promising young Waite Hoyt enabled the Sox to be at least a "respectable" second division ball club. But the end of the season saw another defection to New York. Field manager Barrow was happy to accept an offer to become business manager for the Yankees, enabling him to get away from Frazee and climb on board with the up-and-coming Bronx Bombers. Then, to further anger the fans, Frazee dealt future star hurler Waite Hoyt and catcher Wally Schang to, once again, the Yankees.

For those who might be wondering what number or numbers Stuffy wore in his big league career, the answer is none. It wasn't until 1929 when – who else? – the New York Yankees introduced the idea of putting numerals on the backs of players' jerseys. Babe Ruth was issued number 3 because he almost always batted third in the lineup. Number 4 went to Lou Gehrig, who followed him in the cleanup spot.

The 1921 season displayed Stuffy at his best in his long and productive career. Now 30, and with 12 big league seasons behind him, Stuffy regained his .300 batting form. He played in all but two of the Sox games, going 179 for 584, a .307 batting clip, the leading average on the team that year. But it was at first base, with his little round glove, that he did the best work of his life. He was charged with only one error over the entire season, for an almost unbelievable .999 fielding average. And that lone error was, in the opinion of Aaron Davis and Paul Rogers III of the "Baseball Biography Project," a highly debatable decision by the official scorer. It occurred on May 31 at Fenway Park. With Jimmy Dykes of the Philadelphia Athletics on first base, the Boston catcher tried to pick him off. As Dykes got safety back to the bag, the ball popped out of Stuffy's glove, and the scorer ruled an error. Dykes claimed that it didn't matter whether the ball was dropped or not, since he was safe anyway, and he afterwards loved to tease Stuffy about it whenever the two got together on the ball field. Once again the Red Sox finished fifth under new manager Hugh Duffy. In 2007, Kevin Youkilis of the Red Sox, a third baseman who proved he could switch to first base and field just as well, broke Stuffy's record for most consecutive games without an error by a first sacker, 119. But after that one questionable call, Stuffy started a new string of perfection for consecutive fielding chances by a first baseman without a bobble, 1,700. It took him two seasons to set that record. Unfortunately, he wouldn't do it while wearing a Boston uniform in 1922. Frazee was shipping a lot of players out of town. Another fan favorite, Stuffy McInnis, was the next to depart, only this time it wasn't to the team he might have preferred to join, the Yankees.

As for Harry Frazee, before the end of the 1923 season, with a push from Ban Johnson, he sold the Boston club to a group headed by J. Robert "Bob" Quinn and headed for New York and his true love, Broadway theater. His reward came when "No, No, Nanette" opened to critical acclaim and sold out houses. After that, the quickest way to start a fight in the Fenway Park grandstand was to hum a few bars of "Tea for Two," the catchy little national hit song from that production, especially if a surviving member of the Royal Rooters was within earshot. "Tessie" was heard no more at Fenway until the Dropkick Murphys celebrated the Sox 21st century triumphs by recording a new version of the Rooters' old theme song.

CLEVELAND, THE RECORD, AND BACK TO BOSTON, BUT NOT FENWAY

"His wife balked at leaving the Boston area, so McInnis signed with the Braves"
  – Quoted by Rick Huhn in 'The Sizzler'

I n the week before Christmas of 1921, baseball's "hot stove league" enthusiasts awoke to the news that the Boston Red Sox had traded their peerless first baseman, Stuffy McInnis, to the Cleveland Indians for three players, George Burns, Joe Harris and Elmer Smith. It was the second time the great first baseman had been traded for three players. That was anything but good news to Stuffy and Elsie, comfortable in their new Manchester home. A disgusted Stuffy let it be known that he was so unhappy with the development that he might even refuse to report to Cleveland for the 1922 season. The sports section of *The New York Times* on Thursday, Dec. 21 included a story headlined "M'Innis And Smith Balk On Big Trade." Datelined Manchester, Mass., Dec. 21, a *Times* writer reported: "A possible hitch in the deal by which John ('Stuffy') McInnis of this town, first baseman for the Boston Americans, was to be transferred to the Cleveland Club for three other players developed today with McInnis' statement that he did not intend to join the Indians." The story quoted Stuffy as claiming he could not be transferred without his approval. The *Times* also noted that Elmer Smith was equally unhappy, terming the trade "an injustice."

Angry though Stuffy may have been with the Boston management, he really had no leverage to fight the deal. While today's star players may enjoy long-term contracts that may even include no-trade clauses or the right to veto a trade, ballplayers of Stuffy's day had no such perks. They were held in thrall by baseball's "Reserve Clause," which bound a player's rights to his present team even after the season ended and his one-year contract expired. That clause had been upheld by Kenesaw Mountain Landis while he was a federal judge, a factor that might have contributed to the owners' willingness to appoint him to the new post of Baseball Commissioner, even though the judge demanded and won almost dictatorial authority. Stuffy had only two choices. He could accept the deal and report to Cleveland, or he could retire as an active player, stay in Manchester, and figure out what he was going to do with the rest of his life after having devoted all of his time and effort to baseball. Stuffy was 31 and still at his peak as a player. Quitting the sport at that time seemed like a poor choice, so he had to swallow his anger and move on. On Christmas Eve, an announcement was made that the trade was now official. We presume that Elsie stayed behind in Manchester much of the time while her husband was making his living beside Lake Erie. Since their marriage she had been used to him departing on road trips with the Sox, but after a week or two he'd be home. Now she would have to get along without him for six months, except when the Indians came to Boston for a series of games and he could take the train home to Manchester in the evening.

The Cleveland Indians in 1922 were managed by the future Hall of Famer Tris Speaker, a star center fielder for the Red Sox from 1910-15 when he played between Duffy Lewis and Harry Hooper before being traded to Cleveland. Named the Indians manager in 1919, he continued to play the outfield while piloting the team. The Indians won the 1920 World Series despite the tragic death earlier in the season of shortstop Ray Chapman after he was hit in the head by a Carl Mays pitch, but fell off the pace in '21. Hopes were high that the Tribe could regain the top in '22. But as it turned out, the team finished a disappointing fourth in the American League, just two games over .500. Author Timothy M. Gay, in his biography "Tris Speaker – the Rough and Tumble Life of a Baseball Legend," wrote this about the 1922 Indians: "Not even the acquisition of Speaker's old rival Stuffy McInnis could prevent a slide toward mediocrity." The Indians played at the old League Park, and according to *Baseball-Reference.com*, drew 528,145 paying customers, fifth in attendance among the eight AL clubs. Yet if Stuffy had been furious about the trade, he did not let it affect his performance on the field for his new team. Installed by Speaker at his usual position, first base, McInnis played 140 of the 154 games in the field, and also appeared twice as a pinch hitter. With 164 hits and 78 RBI, he batted a lusty .305, almost equaling the .307 his last year with the Red Sox. In the field, he continued his stellar level of play. After being charged with that lone questionable error in Boston the season before, Mr. McInnis began a new errorless streak that carried over into the 1922 season. He played 119 consecutive errorless games and handled 1,700 consecutive chances without a miscue. Finally, on June 2, he was charged with his first error since the previous May 31. He ended the season with just 5 miscues for an enviable .997 fielding average. Nobody could accuse Stuffy McInnis of sloughing off from the consistent pace he had set over his major league career, or of not earning every dollar of his salary.

While no written evidence has come to light that there was any bad blood between Speaker and McInnis, the end result cannot help but indicate that they didn't hit it off very well. There seems no other explanation for the Indians' decision to get rid of Stuffy before the 1923 season. Perhaps Speaker still harbored a grudge over Stuffy's reluctance to accept the trade to Cleveland, although as a manager who wanted to win, it hardly made sense that he wouldn't want to keep such a talented player who lived cleanly and proved durable. It certainly wasn't the start of a youth movement, since the new Cleveland first baseman in 1923 was 30 years old.

But for whatever the reason, on Feb. 21, 1923, just a couple of weeks before the start of spring training, the Indians informed the baseball world that they had just released Stuffy McInnis. It seems odd from this distance. McInnis was 32, perhaps on the old side for a player of his day but which today usually means a player at the height of his career. He had just come off an outstanding individual season, despite the overall failings of the ball club. Such a player would seem to have considerable trade value, but rather than working out a deal with another club, Cleveland just turned the Gloucester Whaler loose. This left Stuffy in a very unusual position, a talented player who was in effect a free agent, able to work out a deal for himself. There were other free agents looking for work, but those were marginal players who at best could hope to catch on somewhere as a bench warmer. Stuffy was the real thing, but with the season just around the corner, Cleveland hadn't left him much room for negotiating.

According to a passage in "The Sizzler" by Rick Huhn, a 2004 biography of George Sisler, the St. Louis Browns' outstanding pitcher turned first baseman, the Browns made a serious offer to Stuffy to join that team for the '23 season. Sisler was experiencing health problems in the off-season, and nobody was sure whether he'd be ready for the opener in 1923. Stuffy, being available, was an excellent insurance policy should "Gorgeous George" be unable to start the season. But Huhn's account says it was Elsie McInnis who put a stop to the negotiations before they had a chance to get serious. Cleveland had been bad enough, but St. Louis, notorious for its hot Sunday afternoon doubleheaders, was a place Elsie wanted no part of. She loved her home near the ocean, with its cool summer breezes and with family and friends close by. Wrote Huhn (p. 156): "The Browns had taken a serious run at Stuffy McInnis, the slick fielding first baseman of the Philadelphia Athletics and more recently of the Indians... According to the business manager, when the team learned George (Sisler) would be late in arriving, they tried to entice McInnis to join them. His wife balked at leaving the Boston area, so McInnis signed with the Braves." It's easy to speculate that along with respecting Elsie's wishes, Stuffy was well aware that as soon as Sisler made his expected arrival on the scene, Stuffy would be out of a job once more. As it turned out, according to the baseball reference encyclopedia "The Ballplayers," edited by Mike Shatzkin, Sisler was forced to miss the entire 1923 season with a nerve condition that caused him to experience double vision, so "Dutch" Schliebner, a minor leaguer picked up from the Dodgers, filled in for him at first base. Sisler returned in 1924 as player-manager of the Browns with a $25,000 contract. But as spring training began in 1923, Elsie got her wish. Her man was coming home. On March 9 he accepted an offer to sign with the Boston Braves, the National League club that played its home games a mile and a half down Commonwealth Avenue from Fenway Park. The 1917 Sox had used Braves Field for World Series games because of its larger capacity, but by 1923 the Braves were playing before a lot of empty seats. The transaction was officially listed as a "waiver deal" from Cleveland to cover the Reserve Clause, but in reality it was a free agent signing. Having chosen to dump Stuffy in February, the Indians got nothing for him.

Boston's National League franchise dated back to 1871, when the Spalding brothers moved their pioneer professional team, the Red

Stockings, from Cincinnati to Boston. Re-christened the Beaneaters, the team enjoyed success as a member of the old National Association, which became the National League, and the team took the name Braves except for a couple of years in the 1930s when it inexplicably adopted the moniker "Bees." After the earth-shaking World Series sweep of the Athletics in 1914, the Braves entered a down period in which the team dropped into the second division and attendance plunged along with it. But Boston remained a two-team town until 1953, when after a miserable year at the box office in 1952, owner Lou Perini moved the Braves to Milwaukee, the first of the "original 16" to desert its traditional base. After a few good years in the beer capital, the team was sold again in 1965 and moved to Atlanta, leaving Milwaukee fans in the lurch until they got the Brewers in 1970.

If the Red Sox had descended into mediocrity in the wake of the fire sales to the Yankees, Boston's other pro franchise was in tatters. The Braves of 1922 had finished in the National League cellar. The team needed a first baseman, since Walter Holke, who had played the bag in 1922, wouldn't be back and there were no rookie "phenoms" on the horizon. Now a popular homegrown ballplayer with spotless credentials at that position was suddenly available, with no need to give up anyone in trade for him. Stuffy must have been as delighted as Elsie when the offer from Boston came along as spring training was about to begin. In the 1924 directory for Manchester, the occupation for John P. McInnis of 11 Tappan Street (Manchester listings were published only on alternate years in the Beverly Directory) was listed proudly as Professional ballplayer, Boston National League Club. It was a big adjustment for Stuffy. Since his first signing by Connie Mack as a teenager in Beverly, he had played his entire career in the American League. He saw "senior circuit" clubs only at World Series time. Now he had to get used to unfamiliar pitchers from the New York Giants, Brooklyn Dodgers, Philadelphia Phillies, Pittsburgh Pirates, Cincinnati Reds, Chicago Cubs and St. Louis Cardinals. But baseball was baseball, and Stuffy, a seasoned professional, would adjust. Best of all, he was back home.

The Braves in 1923 were managed by Fred Mitchell, a former pitcher who came in to relieve the immortal Cy Young when the Boston American League team (then called the Pilgrims) played its debut game with the infant league in 1901. He had, of course, managed the Chicago Cubs against the Sox in 1918. Three long, hard years as skipper of the Braves were enough for him, but after leaving the pro ranks he held for 12 years the same college coaching job that Stuffy McInnis eventually succeeded to. The '23 Braves, having just finished last, were hardly an outfit to worry the rest of the National League. The starting pitchers, lefty Rube Marquard, Jesse Barnes and Joe Genewich, were at least decent, winning almost as many games as they lost for a bad club. The relief pitching, for the most part, was horrible. Future manager Billy Southworth, 30, who batted .319 with 195 hits, anchored the outfield. The infield included such forgettable figures as Hod Ford, Bob Smith and Tony Boeckel. But at least Mitchell now had a real first baseman and could say, "That's the Stuff, Kid" as he penciled McInnis into the starting lineup, day after day, every day. For the first and only time in his career, Stuffy played every game on the schedule, doubleheaders included, never asking out for an injury or any other reason. Mitchell didn't have to worry about the old veteran being tossed out of a game by an umpire, and as far as we know Stuffy never was ejected during his playing career.

Stuffy repaid the manager's trust with another stellar season. If anyone in Cleveland still thought Mr. McInnis was about washed up as a player, Stuffy disabused them of that notion. Over the 154 game season, the 32-year-old was credited with 607 official at bats and banged out a career high 191 hits along with 95 runs batted in, the most since his 101 in 1912. All but 34 of his hits were singles, as the little guy continued to spray the ball around to all fields and reach base. He batted .315, just four points behind team leader Southworth, who missed only one game all season. Despite facing unfamiliar pitching he continued to be one of the hardest men in baseball to strike out, fanning only 12 times over the course of the April to October season. Defensively he slipped a little bit from his record years of 1921-22, committing 14 errors in 1,603 chances. Some of those might be chalked up to playing on unfamiliar fields. Whatever the Braves paid him, they got a bargain. It wasn't a good year financially for the team, as it drew only 227,802 paying customers into Braves Field, last in the National League. The Braves were horrible again, losing 100 of their 154 games. At least this time they finished seventh, not last, although that was small consolation. Over the winter their long-suffering fans could remember the achievements of Southworth and good old Stuffy McInnis, the hometown boy.

If the 1923 Braves were nothing to cheer about, things got no better in 1924. A new manager, Dave Bancroft, took over from the beleaguered Mitchell, but the team lost 100 games once again while winning one less, 53 (one meaningless game at the end of the season was canceled). The Braves fell to eighth place once more, and attendance at their home games actually fell to 177,487, an average of less than 2,500 per game.

Jesse Barnes pitched gallantly, winning 15 games with an earned run average of 3.23, but he lost 20 times as his mates could give him little support. Stuffy kept his regular first base position under Bancroft, and once again gave his best to his new manager, his teammates and the loyal fans who did show up to rattle around in the almost empty stands. He played 146 games, and although his batting average slipped to .291, he nevertheless contributed 169 hits and 59 RBI, striking out only 6 times for a career low to show that his batting eye was as good as ever. He even improved on his fielding average to .994, committing just 10 errors in the 146 games.

Stuffy had a new teammate on the '24 Braves, a colorful veteran outfielder on the down side of his career named Charles Dillon Stengel, nicknamed "Casey" because he originally haled from Kansas City. Stengel was regarded as what in later years would be termed a "flake." His most legendary exploit as a ballplayer occurred in 1919 when he was playing for Pittsburgh against his old team, the Brooklyn Dodgers, at Ebbets Field. The Brooklyn crowd was really getting on Casey that day. At one point one of the relief pitchers caught a sparrow that had been hopping around the bullpen area and handed it to Stengel in the dugout. Casey put the bird under his cap just before he walked to home plate for his turn at bat. As the crowd booed him, Stengel made an elaborate bow and doffed his cap, letting the bird fly out. The fans gasped, roared with laughter, and then gave old Case a big cheer. Stengel later managed the Braves for three years in the '30s, but his real legend began in 1949 when the Yankees summoned him from the minors to take over as manager for Bucky Harris, who was fired after the team dropped to third place in 1948. In 12 seasons leading the Bronx Bombers, Stengel won 10 pennants and five consecutive World Series titles. Equipped with a roster of stars, he also won by platooning players at certain positions and was the first manager to employ a specialized "closer" out of the bullpen, "Fireman" Joe Page. Dismissed as too old after the Yanks lost the 1960 World Series to Pittsburgh, Stengel went home to be vice president of his bank in Glendale, Calif., but was lured back to New York in '62 as manager of the amazingly inept expansion Mets (40-120, leading Casey to ask, "Can anybody here play this game?") Stuffy, in later years, could tell people he played with Stengel way back when.

Stuffy must have spent the off-season home in Manchester looking forward to another start of spring training and hoping that the Braves management could make some moves to shore up the weak lineup and bring the fans back to Braves Field. But when the financially strapped team offered him a pay cut, he was in no hurry to report as usual to spring training in March of 1925. And he never got the chance to take the field on opening day after the Braves broke camp and headed north. The club had to make some moves and perhaps cut payroll. Stuffy was 34 now, and in those days of shorter life spans, 34 was considered old for a ballplayer. On April 13 he was told for the second time in his career that he was being released. If the lowly Boston Braves no longer wanted him, it appeared he must go home and face up to the possibility that his long professional baseball career might finally be over.

A LAST HURRAH IN PITTSBURGH

"Put Stuffy in there!"

    – John McGraw to Bill McKechnie, 1925 World Series

B ack home in Manchester without a job in baseball for the first time since he turned professional at 17, Stuffy could only contemplate life as a "free agent." In this day and age, a player who has been released can have his agent make calls to teams all around the majors to see if anyone is interested in his client's services, and to negotiate a possible deal. Stuffy had no such advocate. His release would have been announced on baseball's "wire," letting all of the other 15 clubs know he could be signed without giving up any players or cash to the Braves. He could, of course, have chosen just to retire and contemplate another line of work, or perhaps try to hook on somewhere as a coach. But with the season already under way, the latter option was doubtful indeed. He had a family to support, as Elsie had presented him with a little daughter they named Eileen, their only child. Baseball was what Stuffy knew, and the competitive fires that had sustained him for so long had not burned out. He knew he could still help a major league ball club. Maybe a team would lose a first baseman to injury or suspension, or a manager dissatisfied with the talent he had might see a proven old timer as a smart acquisition. While Stuffy wasn't a home run hitter, he was a career .300 batter and he had perhaps the best batting eye in the game. Just the past year with the Braves he had struck out only 6 times in 611 plate appearances, an unbelievable achievement that bettered his 9 K's for the 1921 Red Sox. Moreover, few if any first basemen were his equal around the bag. All he could do was put the word out that he was available, then wait and see.

He'd have to wait for six frustrating weeks. But then fortune struck and Stuffy was back in the game. Bill McKechnie, manager of the Pittsburgh Pirates, had a promising young first baseman in George Grantham, a solid hitter, whom the team had obtained in a trade with the Chicago Cubs. But Grantham had been a second baseman for the Cubs and now was being converted to a first sacker. He definitely needed work on his defensive game, so having an experienced backup on hand was just plain good insurance. Would Mr. McInnis be interested in the job, especially since the Pirates bid fair to contend for the National League pennant? Indeed Stuffy was, and on May 29 he signed a contract to join Pittsburgh. While Elsie might have preferred that he stay home, she had married a professional baseball player, and during the spring and summer months professional baseball players went wherever the job took them. At least Pittsburgh was nearer than St. Louis, and perhaps not as hot in July. If she chose, she could stay in Manchester and care for her little daughter.

So Stuffy packed his suitcase along with his trusty first baseman's glove, boarded the train and joined his new team, the fifth he had played for since his major league debut. He would of course have to get used to a new role. For the past 14 seasons, since taking over for the aging Jasper Davis as a 20-year-old and becoming part of Connie Mack's "$100,000 Infield," Stuffy had been an every day first baseman with, judging by today's standards, all-star credentials. Now he had to resume the role he had played in 1910, as a reserve who would enter the game when called on – maybe today, maybe tomorrow, maybe not till next week. It was a step back in his career, but at least he was still drawing a big league paycheck. And he found himself part of a team that was making the National League sit up and take notice. The New York Giants of John McGraw had been a dominant force in the senior circuit, but the 1925 Pirates were poised to dethrone them. Of the starting nine, only second baseman Eddie Moore failed to hit .300, and he came ever so close at .298. In the outfield, center fielder Kiki Cuyler batted a sterling .357 with 18 home runs and an astonishing 220 hits in 153 games, old pro switch hitter Max Carey was close behind at .343, and Clyde Barnhart chipped in with .325. Pie Trainor at third base rapped the baseball at a .320 clip, and young shortstop Glenn Wright (.308) also smashed 18 homers. Catcher Earl Smith and his backup Johnny Gooch combined to hit .300. Grantham batted a lusty .326, but he played in just 114 games. McKechnie called on Stuffy 59 times, either at first base or as a pinch hitter, and the old veteran proved how wise a move his signing had been by collecting 57 hits in 155 at bats, for a team-leading average of .368. His amazing batting eye hadn't diminished a bit, as he struck out only once in those 59 games. On defense he continued to sparkle, committing just three errors for a .993 average, four points better than Grantham, who must have absorbed some tips along the way from his distinguished backup.

And if the Pirates' hitting skills were frightening to the rest of the National League, the Bucs' pitching staff was downright terrifying. At that time when it was considered a mark of distinction for a team to have four starting pitchers, the Pirates boasted five, and all of them were sterling performers on the mound that year: Lee Meadows (19-10), Ray Kremer (17-8), Emil Yde (the only lefty, 17-9), Johnny Morrison (17-14) and Vic Aldridge (15-7). McKechnie seldom had to go to his bullpen for a relief pitcher, and when he did, 43-year-old Charles "Babe" Adams, a Pirate since 1909, shuffled in with his bag of tricks and contributed 6 wins to the cause against 5 losses. The team's other three relievers went a combined 4-4. When the regular season was over, the Pirates won 95 games while losing only 58 to take the National League flag. They scored 912 runs against their opponents' 715, and drew 804,354 enthusiastic fans to their home park, Forbes Field, to lead the league in attendance. They'd go into the World Series against the 1924 world champions, the Washington Senators, who were led by their legendary pitcher, the "Big Train" Walter Johnson. For the sixth time in his career, Stuffy was part of a World Series team. Twice he'd had to sit out, once in 1910 as a raw 19-year-old, and the following year due to an injury. Twice he had played disappointingly, before chipping in strongly for the 1918 Red Sox. Now he had to wonder whether he would get another chance to be a hero, or just be primarily a bench warmer leading the cheers?

That 1925 World Series turned out to be one of the most exciting since the fall classic was launched in 1903. It began on October 7, with

55

41,723 spectators crammed into Forbes Field to watch the show. And now the rest of the country could follow the action as it happened. Before the advent of commercial radio broadcasts, there was only one way for fans outside the park to keep up with the game. A telegrapher seated in the press box tapped out brief summaries as play proceeded, sending those reports by Morse Code out over the wire. Scoreboards were set up in the front windows of newspaper offices in many cities, and at favorite taverns before Prohibition. Fans, who could get away from work or school, gathered on the sidewalk. As play developed, a receiving telegrapher handed messages to copyboys, who rushed out to post the latest updates. Sometimes the boy was also given a megaphone, allowing him to shout a bit of play-by-play. But by 1925, commercial radio stations were springing up all over, with KDKA in Pittsburgh being one of the first to send its signal out far and wide to those who could buy or build a receiver set. For the '25 series, Graham McNamee brought his microphone into both Forbes Field and Washington's Griffith Stadium, to describe the action live over the new Westinghouse Radio Network. Umpires chosen to work the series were Cy Rigler and Barry McCormack from the National League, and Brick Owens and George Moriarty from the junior circuit. Bill McKechnie, nicknamed "Deacon," had been the Pirates manager since 1922, never finishing below third place. The Senators were directed by player-manager Bucky Harris, the team's regular second baseman. Washington, once a doormat, had made a splash in 1924 by not only winning the American League pennant, but also following up by upsetting the heavily favored New York Giants in the World Series. The Giants beat Johnson twice, but in the seventh game the old veteran "Big Train" came out of the bullpen in relief and ended up as the winning pitcher.

For the opener in Pittsburgh, to nobody's surprise, Harris went with his ace, Johnson, while McKechnie countered with 19-game winner Lee Meadows. Johnson was at his best, allowing the Bucs just one run on a Pie Trainor homer in the bottom of the fifth, as the Senators jumped out in front with a 4-1 victory on the road. Stuffy McInnis had feared he might be left out, and that was indeed the case, as McKechnie penciled the 25-year-old Grantham onto the lineup card at first base instead of his veteran, who had now turned 35. McInnis would have to root his teammates on from his seat in the dugout. He again sat for game two, when Vic Aldridge faced Washington's number two pitcher, Stan Coveleski. It was a stirring pitchers' duel for 7½ innings until the Pirates struck for two runs in the bottom of the eighth. The Senators got one back in the top of the ninth, but Aldridge hung on for a 3-2 complete game win, and the series was tied.

With the action switching to Griffith Stadium on October 11 and 36,495 on hand, the Senators managed 10 hits off Ray Kremer and took a one game lead in the series by edging the Bucs, 4-3. Alex Ferguson picked up the win for the boys from the nation's capital, with Firpo Marberry relieving him in the eighth to earn a save. The contest produced a very controversial play in the top half of the eighth inning when Washington right fielder Sam Rice dove into the bleachers to rob catcher Earl Smith of a game-tying home run. Pittsburgh argued loud and long that it wasn't a catch, and that a Senators fan might have put the ball into Rice's glove before he emerged from the stands. The umpires stuck to the "out" call. (In a 1965 sealed letter to the Baseball Hall of Fame, not to be opened until after his death, Rice wrote: "At no time did I lose possession of the ball.") That loss put the Pirates in a hole and left them in a "must win" situation for game four. But they had to face Walter Johnson, and the "Big Train" totally mastered Pittsburgh's heavy hitting lineup, shutting them out while the Senators got to Emil Yde for four runs in the third inning, all they needed for a 4-0 win and a 3-1 lead in the series. McKechnie called on 43-year-old Babe Adams to pitch the eighth inning, and the old man was up to the task, but by then the game was lost. No team had ever come back from a 3-1 deficit to win a World Series, so the Pirates faced a seemingly insurmountable deficit.

As for Stuffy, he had sat out all four games, making just one appearance off the bench as a pinch hitter in game four for Johnny Morrison, who had relieved Yde after his third inning blowup. He must have seethed as he watched George Grantham flail away futilely at Washington pitching, going just 2 for 15 and a .133 batting average, with three strikeouts. He hadn't exactly sparkled in the field, either. John McGraw, the fiery long-time manager of the New York Giants, was in attendance at the series. McGraw, who hated the American League and its president Ban Johnson with a passion, was still gnashing his teeth over the Giants' loss to the Senators the year before. Now the Washington upstarts were on the verge of humiliating the senior circuit for the second year in a row, and McGraw was in one of his rages. The story is that after game four, McGraw stormed into the Pirates' clubhouse to confront McKechnie. "What's the matter with you? You're playing that bum Grantham when you've got the best first baseman in baseball sitting on your bench. Put Stuffy in there!" Whether it was anything to do with McGraw or whether McKechnie had come to the same conclusion, when he made out the lineup for game five, still at Griffith Stadium on October 12, McInnis was at first base and Grantham was on the bench. Stuffy's presence on the field seemed to calm the jittery Pirates, who disappointed another sellout home crowd of 35,899 by breaking open what had been a close game with a 6-3 victory. Pittsburgh's hitherto feeble bats finally came alive with a 13-hit attack that chased Coveleski in the seventh inning, and they kept up the attack against three relievers.

With the Pirates still alive, the teams boarded the train to return to Pittsburgh and game six the next day, October 13. The conversation aboard the evening train must have been lively, with the Pirates out to convince themselves they could still win the series. There was also no doubt that Stuffy McInnis would be at first base once again. With their hopes renewed, 43,810 fans poured into Forbes Field for game six. Things started out grimly for the home team, as the Senators jumped out to a 2-0 lead against Ray Kremer with runs in each of their first two at-bats. But Kremer settled down to blank the visitors the rest of the way. The Pirates tied the game in the bottom of the third, and went ahead to stay when Eddie Moore homered in the bottom of the fifth to provide a 3-2 lead, which was the final score. Stuffy again anchored the infield. Suddenly, the series was tied. After a day off on the 14th, the teams were to play a seventh and deciding game on the 15th. Stuffy, of course, was back in the lineup. But the Pirates had to face Walter Johnson, who'd stopped them cold twice.

When the Senators chased Vic Aldridge out of the game with a four-run outburst in the top of the first, it appeared as though Pittsburgh's hopes for a historic comeback were as dead as a fish two days out of water. Not so fast. The Pirates cut the margin to 4-3 in the bottom of the third, only to see Washington go right out and extend the lead to 6-3 with their next time at bat. But the great Walter Johnson was tiring, and by the seventh inning Pittsburgh tied the game 6-6 as more than 42,000 fans roared approval. Despite Johnson's obvious weariness, Harris let him come back to the mound in the eighth. The grateful Pirates took advantage, scoring three times and running their hit total to 15 on the way to a 9-7 triumph. The '25 Pittsburgh team had done the hitherto impossible, coming back from a 3-1 deficit to win the World Series, defeating one of the game's greatest legends in the deciding game. According to *Baseball Almanac*, a livid Ban Johnson chastised Harris for letting the weary Johnson finish the game, telling Bucky: "You sacrificed a world's championship for our league through your display of mawkish sentiment." The Pirates didn't mind in the least that the great pitcher had suffered a meltdown when it most helped their cause.

As for Stuffy, he ended up with 4 hits in 14 at bats (4 for 13 over the last three games), an average of .286, with one run batted in. Ironically, it was his best batting average in the four World Series in which he had played an important role. Perhaps more importantly, he had helped in a big way to settle down his mates in the field at a time when it appeared the series was lost. Mr. McInnis had started the 1925 season sitting at home in Manchester after having been released by arguably the worst team in baseball. Now he could go home for the winter a world champion once again. McKechnie and the Pirates offered him the chance to return for the 1926 season, again in the role of substitute, and he accepted. George Grantham, shaking off his weak performance in October, was now settling in as the every day first baseman, doubtless with the coaching and encouragement of Stuffy, who got off the bench fewer times in 1926. While playing in only 47 of the team's 154 games, he nevertheless batted .299, eight points shy of his career average. Hopes were high in Pittsburgh for another first place run, but the team stumbled down the stretch and ended up third. With the season over, Stuffy, now 36, knew his playing days were finished at last. But he'd have one more shot at the big time, as a manager.

THE PHILLIES MANAGER COMES HOME – WHICH WITCH?

"Where would a circus in Salem locate now?"
  – Salem Evening News, July 17, 1921

Even though Stuffy McInnis had to face that the end of the 1926 season meant the end of his long major league playing career, there was another year for him in the "big show." Having put together a stellar record while building his reputation as a clean-living, smart, dependable team player, Stuffy certainly was a prime candidate to become a manager, either in the major leagues or a top minor circuit. After all, he had learned from playing for such luminaries as Connie Mack and Ed Barrow. He soon got an offer. The Philadelphia Phillies, who had fallen to the basement of the National League, were looking for a new field leader for the 1927 season. Stuffy McInnis signed a contract with Phillies owner William F. Baker, for whom the team's home park, Baker Bowl, was named. "That's the Stuff Kid" had started his major league career in Philadelphia in 1909 at the tender age of 18; now he was returning to the City of Brotherly Love at 36 in a brand new role. If that was where his big league days were destined also to end, so be it. To assist him as coaches Stuffy selected Dan Murphy, his former outfield teammate with the A's; and canny old former catcher Joe Sugden, who had played for five big league clubs and had been a teammate of and backup catcher for Connie Mack back in 1895.

While no evidence for this appears, it is easy to speculate that Stuffy might have paid a courtesy call on his old mentor Mack. He had watched the master's managerial strategy for nine seasons, picking up a lot of inside baseball knowledge along the way, and now that he was a manager himself he must have been anxious to seek out any advice that Mack was willing to impart. There was no reason for Mack to deny him some tips, since odds-makers of the time would have laughed at any suggestion that the Athletics and Phillies might face each other that October. If the two men did meet, they did so as old friends who were now colleagues.

Stuffy can't have accepted his new responsibility with any illusions that he could turn the lowly Phillies from losers into winners. Those who follow baseball closely might agree that over the course of a season a good manager may, by making the right moves, pulling the right strings, playing the right hunches, win four or five games for his team that would otherwise have been lost. But it's the players who have to execute. The manager makes out the lineup card, decides when to change pitchers and make substitutions, employs some game strategy, and hopes for the best. He can put on the sign for a hit-and-run play, or a sacrifice bunt, or a pick-off, and if it works out, he looks good. If his players mess it up, the fans call the manager a bum. With a good team in a close pennant race, those four or five games can make the difference between finishing first or being also-rans. Good players generally make good managers. Stuffy's 1924 teammate with the Braves, Casey Stengel, could attest to that. When he managed the Yankees for 12 seasons from 1949-1960, he not only had star hitters, fielders and pitchers, he also had some talented players on his bench to allow him to employ a bit of cunning substitution strategy along with the day to day platooning of players at certain positions that made him famous. His teams won 10 pennants, and he was dismissed only after the 1960 club lost the World Series. But after a year in his banker's office in California, when he was lured back to New York to manage the 1962 expansion Mets, it was a different story. Through an "expansion draft," the other National League owners had stuck the Mets with a collection of washed-up veterans, "flakes" and discards, leaving Stengel with the impossible task of putting a competitive team on the field. That year the Mets finished 40-120, for a .250 winning percentage. Fortunately for the management, the team was so bad that National League fans in New York, delighted to have their favorite league back in the Big Apple after a bitter five-year absence, took the Mets to their hearts as "loveable losers." They turned out to cheer for "Marvelous Marv" Throneberry and his bumbling mates as they figured out new ways to lose games that drew colorful comments from the frustrated Stengel when the reporters crowded around him. They jeered the opposition, especially when the "turncoat" Giants and Dodgers, who had de-camped for the West Coast after the 1957 season, came to town. It was unheard of for New Yorkers to love a loser, but for that crazy summer, they did. Stengel was retired again when the 1969 Mets not only won the National League pennant, but also took the World Series from the heavily favored Baltimore Orioles, who until 1954 had been the St. Louis Browns. It's an axiom in baseball that when a team's performance fails to meet front office expectations, the solution is to fire the manager. The Mets owners didn't dare to fire Casey, so it took a fall and a broken hip to bring him down.

The Phillies were losers, but did not fit the "loveable" category, and their fans had grown tired of losing. Their new manager could not have been optimistic as he met with his coaches to try to figure out some ways to turn things around. The starting pitchers McInnis had available – 35-year-old Jack Scott, Alex Ferguson, Dutch Ulrich, Hub Pruett and Wes Sweetland – hardly constituted a staff that would strike fear into National League opposition. None of them won 10 games in that long season, with Scott coming "closest" at 9-21. Among them they lost 75 games while winning only 34. And the Phillies had little to offer any other teams for trades to try to improve. The starting lineup – catcher Jimmie Wilson, an infield of Russ Wrightstone, Fresco Thompson, shortstop Heinie Sand and Bernie Friberg, and an outfield of Freddie Leach, Dick Spalding and Cy Williams – included a couple of recognizable names, but was hardly a stellar collection. The bench players were a group of unknowns. Stuffy certainly couldn't impersonate Connie Mack, or John McGraw, or Bill McKechnie either, with those guys.

The Phillies stumbled out of the gate, and things only got worse as they descended to their anticipated place in the National League cellar. They weren't quite as bad as the '62 Mets, but managed to lose 103 games while winning only 51, for a .331 percentage, finishing nine games in back of the still-sad seventh place Boston Braves, and a telescopic 43 games behind the pennant winning Pirates, who had regained their 1925 touch after the '26 disappointment to edge out the St. Louis Cardinals and McGraw's Giants in a close race for the flag. (They'd fall to Babe Ruth and the mighty Yankees in the World Series.) The Phillies allowed 903 runs while scoring only 678. Only 305,420 loyal but unhappy fans paid their way into Baker Bowl, putting the Phils next to last in the league for attendance. About the only highlight of the season came on August 5, when Cy Williams performed the rare feat of hitting for the "cycle" in four consecutive at-bats, meaning that he collected a home run, a triple, a double and a single.

Unlike Connie Mack, Stuffy managed the team in uniform, permitting him to leave the dugout to confer with a pitcher or an umpire. And although he was strictly a bench manager, unlike Speaker or Harris who doubled as a player, he actually entered a contest himself one final time. On Aug. 1, in the last inning, he pulled out his trusty old glove and inserted himself into the game at first base. No account of that game is available without a time-consuming search. So we don't know whether Stuffy's decision to play was out of necessity, out of a wish to show his listless team that their manager was unafraid to go out there, or just out of a desire to see his name again in a box score. He didn't get to bat, but the record shows that he had one put-out at first base. That token appearance had the result of entering his name into the 1927 record book, adding a 19th season to his major league playing career. The one put-out gave him a perfect 1.000 fielding average for the year, a point "better" than his incredible .999 season for the Red Sox in 1921. When October mercifully brought an end to the Phillies' woeful campaign, both Stuffy and Baker were in agreement that he wouldn't return for a second try to right the ship. For 1928 the Phillies turned to Burt Shotten, a Connie Mack clone who managed in a business suit. Shotten found fame almost two decades later, when he managed the 1947 Brooklyn Dodgers, the year of Jackie Robinson's debut, to a National League pennant.

So Stuffy came home to Manchester and Elsie, his major league days at an end. He would, however, have one more go-around at the professional level, on a local basis and in the league he had started his pro days with. The mid-level Class B New England League, dating back to 1886, in which Stuffy had drawn his first pro pay check in 1908, had been reborn in 1926 with teams in eight cities. Salem, Mass. obtained a franchise in 1927. That team, not surprisingly named the Witches, was in need of a manager for the 1928 season. Stuffy, having shaken off the dust of the disastrous season with the Phillies, was home in nearby Manchester and was available. Perhaps making the job all the more attractive to him was that he was allowed to be a player-manager. A B league such as the New England was, of course, primarily intended as a training ground for up and coming baseball hopefuls. Stuffy wouldn't want to, or be expected to, perform as an every day player, but when he wished he could write his name in the lineup and try to recapture a bit of his youth.

Besides Salem, the franchises active for 1928 were the Lynn Papooses, Manchester (N.H.) Blue Sox, Lewiston Twins, Brockton Shoemakers, Attleborough Burros, Portland Mariners, and the Haverhill Hillies, a reincarnation of Billy Hamilton's 1908 Haverhill Hustlers for whom Stuffy had performed for two months after it was revealed that Connie Mack was going to sign him. The opposition wasn't entirely led by strangers. The Portland team was managed by Duffy Lewis, the legendary Red Sox left fielder against whom Stuffy had played for several seasons and who had briefly been his teammate. Down at Attleborough was none other than Patsy Donovan, the one-time Boston skipper who was victimized on the day back in 1911 when Stuffy pulled off his "hurry-up home run" stunt. Another old-time star from the turn of the century, Jesse Burkett, for whom a Little League in Worcester is named, managed the Lewiston Twins. All references to the league list the Salem home park as "not available," but the Witches seem certain to have played at a field off Bridge Street that is no longer in existence. The Salem franchise of 1927-28 was owned by local sports promoter Frank Donovan. An article in the July 12, 1921 issue of the *Salem Evening News*, headlined "Where Would a Circus Locate in Salem Now?" reported that the traveling circus that made an annual visit to the city "ain't got no home" since the Bridge Street grounds where the circus formerly set up shop had been leased to Frank Donovan "who will fix it up for a baseball and athletic field." Donovan was as good as his word. A photo of the Bridge Street grounds taken during an exhibition ball game, provided by Nelson Dionne of the Beverly Historical Society's Walker Transportation Group shows a ballpark with a packed grandstand six rows high running the length of the third base line and behind home plate. Donovan sub-leased the field for three years to the Salem High School Athletic Association "for all kinds of athletic games." That location seems to be the same "Bridge Street grounds" located west of the bridge connecting Beverly and Salem where the Salem High School football team played its home games before Bertram Field was built, and where the Beverly-Salem Thanksgiving Day rivalry had its birth. It may also be remembered that when the Dick Madden-Stuffy McInnis team played its second game versus Salem in the 1907 series, the *Saturday Evening Citizen* complained that the Salem grounds were in "terrible shape," pitted by ruts left from the wagons of the recently departed traveling circus. The job of managing the Salem Witches represented a convenient prospect for the man who made his home a few miles away in Manchester, and the road trips were a short drive or train ride. Elsie must have loved that. All of the teams in the New England League at that time were independent, meaning that they were not owned or controlled by any major league club.

A glance at the 1928 Salem Witches roster reveals a host of anonymous ballplayers, some of whom aren't even supplied with first names. But two names jump out, both pitchers – one a 21-year-old right-handed prospect most definitely on the way up the baseball ladder, the other a local guy making his last professional stop. Roy Parmelee, born in 1907, was just a year away from the major leagues. Aware of his great potential, Stuffy made Parmelee the ace of the Witches' staff, using him in 35 games and a team-high 212 innings. Although his won-lost record was a modest 10-18 that year, he had the second most wins of the 13 pitchers Stuffy employed and posted an earned run average of 4.25. Parmelee, obviously, was being watched by major league scouts, which was one reason his manager chose to showcase him. Even then he revealed the one weakness that plagued him through his career – wildness. The 133 walks he allowed were far and away the most on the team. The league statistician did not keep track of the number of batters hit by pitches, but Parmelee later became notorious for the number of batsmen he plunked with his deliveries. Stuffy must have been very pleased when his protégé was invited to spring training with the New York Giants in 1929 and made the team at age 22. Parmelee, whose nickname was "Bud," ended up spending 10 seasons in the major leagues, toiling for the Giants, Cardinals, Cubs and Athletics, pitching a total of 1,120 innings and with a very respectable lifetime record of 59-55. Mike Shatzkin, editor of "The Ballplayers," had this to say: "A hard thrower, Parmelee never achieved his potential because of a lack of control. Not always a regular starter, he nevertheless led the NL four times in hit batsmen and once in bases on balls." Obviously he was one of those pitchers whom opposing hitters hesitated to dig in against. His best season in the majors was 1933, when he won 13 games while losing 8. One of those wins was on July 2, when he hurled a shutout to beat the Cardinals and the legendary Dizzy Dean, 1-0. His control was really on that day as he struck out 13 of the Redbirds while not issuing a single base on balls.

Joe Batchelder, the other noteworthy performer for the Witches, was 29 at the start of that summer, turning 30 in July. He haled from the small town of Wenham, which adjoins both Beverly and Manchester. Although the fact is forgotten now locally, Joe and Stuffy were teammates on the Boston Braves for parts of two seasons. While he was out of organized baseball by 1928, it is obvious the two men stayed in touch. Batchelder might have attended some of the Witches' games and let Stuffy know he was available if needed, or Stuffy might have contacted him. Whatever the case, the record shows that Batchelder pitched in six games for Salem, going 0-2. Joe Batchelder was a little left-handed thrower who according to the *Baseball Almanac* stood only five foot seven and weighed 165 pounds. Joseph Edmond Batchelder was born in Wenham on July 11, 1898, son of T. Wilson and Martha P. Batchelder, and a descendant of one of the families that founded Wenham in the 17th century. His father had a farm off Main Street near the Wenham Cemetery, but the lad was more interested in baseball than farming. The various listings show that he had two brothers, Clarence and Lincoln, and two sisters, Rena and Hulda. He showed enough potential as a young "southpaw" pitcher to earn a minor league contract. The 1923 Wenham directory lists his occupation as "professional ballplayer, Pittsfield team." The Pittsfield team played at Wahconah Park, still in use today as one of the oldest baseball stadiums in the nation. Near the end of that season he was called up by the Braves and made his major league debut on Sept. 29. He appeared four times before the season ended and even got to start once, pitching a complete game to earn what would be his only major league victory, according to the *Baseball Almanac*. The next season, Stuffy's second and last with the Braves, saw Batchelder spending most of the year in the minors. But the Braves summoned him back long enough to pitch in three games as a reliever, posting a respectable earned run average of 3.86, striking out two batters and walking two. He may have started the 1925 season with the Boston club, but after appearing in just four games for a career total of 11 games, 1 win, 0 losses, he was released in May and never returned to the "big time." That year he was listed as single, boarding with his parents in Wenham. By 1927 he was married (Marion P.), and was now living "next door" in Hamilton. His occupation for the last time was given as professional ballplayer, but no team affiliation was specified, making it seem he must be out of a job. After his brief stint with the Witches he gave up any further dreams of baseball glory, as the next listing has him employed as a chauffeur for Bayard Tuckerman Jr. After a decade of driving for Mr. Tuckerman, he was back in Wenham and had gone to work at Beverly's massive United Shoe Machinery Corp. plant, living on Fiske Road in Wenham, close to his boyhood home. Later directories changed his name to J. Edmond Batchelder. The old pitcher lived to be almost 90, passing on May 5, 1989. His burial took place in

Hamilton Cemetery. When gathered with old cronies at the Heavenly Hall of Fame, he could boast that he'd had a perfect 1.000 won-lost record as a big league pitcher. Not many ever did that.

As for Stuffy, he used himself sparingly but effectively as a player, appearing in 38 of the team's 101 games, 32 at first base and the rest apparently as a pinch hitter. Although the competition was less talented than he'd been used to, he must have been happy to show the young fellows he could still play by rapping out 39 hits in 115 at bats for an average of .339, with 7 extra base hits. RBI stats were not kept. Walter Simpson, who was the regular first baseman, hit only .236. Stuffy relieved him there 32 times, committing only 3 errors. But the younger man wasn't bad with the glove, either, also committing only 3 miscues in 476 chances to edge out his boss for fielding percentage, .994 to .990. Stuffy's "workhorse" was outfielder Walter Unglaub, who played all but two of the team's 101 games, led the club in hits and batted .307. When the season was over, the Witches just managed to top the .500 mark, winning 51 and losing 50 to finish in fifth place – not great, but decent. It must have been a lot more fun for Stuffy than the 1927 season in Philadelphia, especially since he got to play himself as well as teach the young fellows what he knew. But he wouldn't get the chance for a repeat performance. The Salem team had not been a financial success, and the franchise went elsewhere in 1929. The league itself was not long for the baseball world. The stock market crash of October 1929, which ushered in the Great Depression caused the New England League to fold in 1930. It was reborn briefly as a mid-level pro loop in 1946 with the end of World War II, when the majors had developed extensive farm systems. The Red Sox put a team in Lynn to play under the lights at Fraser Field. That year the Brooklyn Dodgers had a New England League club in Nashua, N.H. While Jackie Robinson was working his way to the big club at Brooklyn's International League team in Montreal, two other future black all-stars just signed by the Dodgers, pitcher Don Newcombe and catcher Roy Campanella, were making their pro debuts, and helping to break the color barrier in America, with the Nashua team.

For Stuffy McInnis, the close of the 1928 season meant the end of his association with professional baseball as a player and as a manager. But it hardly marked the conclusion of his association with the sport. He still had a lot to give to baseball, and a lot of coaching to do.

THE COLLEGE COACH, FROM NORWICH TO FAIR HARVARD

"McInnis is anything but an executive when he puts on a pair of spikes and a sweat suit, tucks a baseball into his pocket and walks into Briggs Cage"

– Harvard 'Crimson,' Feb. 19, 1949

With his professional baseball days at an end after more than two decades, it is uncertain what Stuffy McInnis did to pass the time in 1929 and 1930. The Manchester Directory listing for 1930 at the Beverly Historical Society has him living as always at 11 Tappen Street, but for the first time since he took up residence there in 1918 no occupation is given. Surely he must have enjoyed spending time at home with Elsie and little Eileen, who was now 5 years old. There would have been ball games to attend and perhaps he began to sample another game he proved most adept at, golf. We do know that on September 8, 1930, he returned to Boston's Braves Field, where he had played for the home team in 1923-24 and revisited when with the Pirates and Phillies in 1925-27, to take part in an "old timers' game" that brought together many of the stars of Boston's ball clubs from the '10s and '20s.

A crowd of 23,632 turned out for the event which included a regular Braves game, a crowd far in excess of what the Braves were drawing in Stuffy's playing days. A newspaper photo taken that day has Stuffy in the third row with Tris Speaker, Bill Carrigan, Jimmy Collins, Hank Gowdy, Harry Hooper, Frank "Home Run" Baker, Patsy Donovan and others. Also playing that day were such past luminaries as Duffy Lewis, Jack Coombs, Hughey Duffy, Ed Walsh, Dick Hoblitzel (who Stuffy replaced as Red Sox first sacker in 1918) , the legendary pitchers Cy Young and "Smoky" Joe Wood, and two of Stuffy's teammates from the great Philadelphia teams, Rube Oldring and Albert "Chief" Bender. It must have been quite a day for reminiscing and swapping tales. Baseball would soon be calling Stuffy back, this time not with professionals but as a wise and patient coach of young collegiate men who played the sport for the pure joy of it. As a lad who dropped out of high school in 1907 to concentrate his energies on the game he most loved and for which he had such ability, Stuffy never had the chance to set foot on a college campus. Now for nearly two-and-a-half decades he'd be welcome as a teacher in academia, starting at Norwich University in Vermont.

Biographical summaries of Stuffy's life all mention his association with Harvard University baseball, a six-year period which can be well documented. Few, however, pay any attention to the coaching he did prior to arriving at Cambridge, probably because of the lack of much information. From 1931 through 1942, he was baseball coach at Norwich, a prestigious military academy. A headline in *The New York Times* in December of 1930 tells us: "Stuffy McInnis To Coach Norwich University Nine." The rest of the story, unfortunately, could not be read online. Directory listings from 1932 all the way to 1946 give McInnis's occupation as "Baseball coach, Norwich University." Doubtless the cadets of Norwich were thrilled and honored to have such a luminary of the baseball world to coach their team, but the fact seems to be long forgotten on campus today. When Anthony A. Mariano, the athletic director at Norwich, was asked to check the archives to see what material there might be on Stuffy's career there, the result was next to nothing in the files, not even a correct name. Mr. Mariano reported that from 1931 through 1942, the baseball coach was "R. McInnis." He had no idea what the "R" stood for, and since Stuffy's full name was John Phalen McInnis, it appears that whoever compiled the records in those long-ago days didn't bother to list the coach's name correctly. Mr. Mariano provided season records that show Stuffy's record as a coach over the 12 seasons of his tenure was 54 wins and 50 losses. His best season was 1936 when the Cadets went 9-0, with a tenth game ending in a tie, probably called because of darkness. With the chilly, late Vermont springs, the baseball team played a short season, usually eight to 12 games. His teams didn't have a winning record until 1935, but after that they were over .500 through 1940. Norwich dropped baseball and other sports from 1943-45, as the students who had not already left school to join our military effort in World War II were preparing to do so. Peace following the surrender of Nazi Germany and Imperial Japan brought the return of baseball to the campus in 1946, but Stuffy was not part of the scene. Joe Garrity took over as Norwich coach that year.

Stuffy did have a baseball coaching job about 1946 and 1947, with younger players at the Brooks School, a private, coeducational college preparatory school for grades 9-12 in North Andover, Mass. But 1948 saw his return to the college ranks with a "temporary" position at Amherst College in Amherst, Mass., not to be confused with the University of Massachusetts in the same community. The highly respected Paul Eckley, one of two coaches who compiled a long tenure at the helm of the Amherst nine, had been there since 1923. (Eckley finally retired in 1965, to be succeeded by Bill Thurston, who remained there in 2010; both are in the College Baseball Hall of Fame.) Now in the winter of 1948 he was suffering the effects of an illness and his doctor insisted that he take the upcoming baseball season off. The "Lord Jeffs" needed a coach to step in until Eckley was fit again. He undoubtedly either knew Stuffy personally or knew his reputation well, and the Manchester resident was happy to accept an invitation to go back to coaching college men, even though he realized it was just a one-year hire. Amherst, along with its stellar academic reputation, has a storied baseball history. In fact, the very first recognized intercollegiate contest took place on July 1, 1859, between Amherst and Williams College of Williamstown, Mass. (The very date of the game helps give the lie once again to the oft-repeated myth that the present school year is a product of the "agricultural economy." Long summer vacations didn't come along until the latter decades of the 19th century, and had nothing to do with farming.) At the same time as the baseball contest, the chess teams representing the two schools got together for a match. The student newspaper, the *Amherst Express*, marked the occasion with a special edition headlined "Williams and Amherst, Base Ball and Chess! Muscle and Mind!!" It was a time when the rowdy old "town ball" rules of the Massachusetts Game were about to be overwhelmed in this state by the much more orderly, modern rules of Alexander Cartwright's New York

Game. Whatever version was employed that day, the result was a one-sided triumph for Amherst. Each team provided a ball for the contest with the winners to keep both, so the historic baseballs resided in the Amherst trophy case. Now, almost 90 years later, Stuffy McInnis stepped in for the ailing Eckley and led the Lord Jeffs to a very successful 10-1 spring campaign, losing only to Yale, champion of the Eastern Intercollegiate League, by a 4-3 score. The impressed and grateful student body voted Stuffy to be an honorary member of the Amherst Class of 1948. Now 57 years old, the "Gloucester Whaler," the teenage Beverly Town Teamer of long ago, at last could say he was a "graduate" of a noted institution of higher learning. The next year he led his new team, the Harvard Crimson, onto the field as an opponent of Amherst.

In the fall of 1948, Harvard University was in the market for a new baseball coach. Dolph Samborski, a successor to Floyd Stahl, who replaced Stuffy's former Braves manager Fred Mitchell at the Harvard helm, had given up coaching baseball after two seasons to devote his full-time attention to the position of director of intramural athletics. Stuffy McInnis, freed from Amherst by the pending return of the recovered Paul Eckley, was a candidate the Harvard athletic authorities could not resist. A story in the *Harvard Crimson* dated October 20, 1948, headlined "McInnis Is Baseball Coach," informed the campus community that "John P. 'Stuffy' McInnis, first baseman of Connie Mack's immortal $100,000 infield, will coach Harvard's baseball team next spring, H.A.A. Director Bill Bingham announced last night." (The initials stand for Harvard Athletic Association, the university's governing sports body.) "McInnis, who played on four world champion teams, has a long college coaching record. He directed the Norwich University team for 14 years, and after a short stay at Brooks School went to Amherst last year, where he ran up an impressive 10-1 record with the Lord Jeffs." (The writer made one error in reporting that Stuffy went to Norwich immediately after departing the majors, when in fact he took up duties there in 1931.)

Harvard is, of course, the oldest school of higher learning in America, having been founded in 1636 as a training ground for ministers and other leaders of the Puritan colony of Massachusetts Bay. It was named for John Harvard, the clergyman who migrated to Boston from England in 1637 and on his death left his substantial library to the new college. Like Amherst, its baseball roots go back nine decades before Stuffy's arrival. The Harvard archives reveal that the first known baseball nine associated with the college was the Lawrence Base Ball Club of 1858, which represented the Lawrence Scientific School, then part of Harvard. What is most interesting is that those pioneers used the rules of the New York Game, developed in 1845 by Alexander Cartwright and his Knickerbocker Base Ball Club in New York City. The nine men to a side, three outs to an inning, 90-foot base paths rules were slow to catch on in the Bay State, which preferred its own crude version known as the Massachusetts Game. As far as is known the first team to play the new rules in Boston was the Tri-Mountain Club of 1857, so the Lawrence/Harvard outfit was right up there with the pioneers. By the time of the Civil War, the Massachusetts Game had been largely replaced by the better aspects and faster team play of the New York innovation. The first real baseball field was laid out on the Cambridge Common in 1863, and Harvard played its first intercollegiate game on June 27 of that year versus Brown at Providence. The first on-campus ball diamond appeared in 1864, while Harvard won its first contest with Yale in 1868, 25-17. Harvard's most important contribution to the game in terms of safety was in 1877 when team captain Frederick W. Thayer (Harvard '78) invented the catcher's mask. Made to his order by a Cambridge tinsmith, the mask was first worn by James A. Tyng when the Harvards played the Live Oaks at Lynn on April 12, 1877. Derided at first as a "bird cage," the mask quickly caught on at all levels of the sport when it was realized how many painful and disfiguring injuries it prevented for those who took on the dangerous position of catcher, and plate umpire, too.

Harvard offered its new coach one big advantage – he wouldn't have to wait for the spring in order to get going. The university had built Briggs Cage, a spacious, dirt-floored high-ceilinged building, which allowed baseball players and other athletes to work out in relative comfort when snow was still on the ground, cold winds were howling or rain was pelting down. As a result, McInnis was able to issue a call for all baseball candidates to turn out for an introductory meeting at the beginning of February 1949. While he appeared for that meeting in a "well-tailored double breasted" business suit, he made it clear to the young baseball hopefuls that he didn't want to be addressed as Mr. McInnis, or even Coach. "Just call me Stuffy," he told the men who had gathered to meet him. That had been the name he answered to since he was younger than the youngest freshmen at Harvard, and that was the name he would continue to go by. An article in the *Harvard Crimson* by Stephen N. Cady, published on February 19, 1949, quoted Athletic Director Bingham as saying the new coach "looked like a bank president" when he walked into the athletic office the previous September to interview for the job. Now 58 and with hair turning gray, he still had as much enthusiasm for the game of baseball and the lads who play it as he did when he himself was an eager teenager. Wrote Cady: "McInnis is anything but an executive when he puts on a pair of spikes and a sweat-suit, tucks a baseball into his pocket and walks into Briggs Cage." The players soon learned that their new coach was both a patient man and a firm believer that his job entailed giving as much individual instruction as time permitted. "'He goes from one player to another,' one pitcher observes, 'regardless of whether that man happens to be a star.'" In Stuffy's own words: "The most obscure boy may be a future great. Take Bob Feller." (Then the star pitcher of the Cleveland Indians and a future Hall of Famer), "There were only 13 boys in his senior class at high school." Stuffy took time to point out that as a 16-year-old playing for Dick Madden's Beverly team, he had been surrounded by Harvard men. "My association with Harvard started then. The 1907 Beverly club had Eddie Grant, Bill Matthews and Eddie Loughlin, all students at Harvard Law School."

Stuffy's arrival at Harvard also attracted attention from the press in his hometown, whose population included a number of Harvard graduates. The weekly *Manchester Cricket* ran a frontpage story on Feb. 18, 1949, headlined "Stuffy Calls Harvard Nine." The story went on to say: "John 'Stuffy' McInnis of Tappan Street, head coach of the Harvard baseball team, recently issued his first call for candidates and has started his men working inside. This is Stuffy's first year with the Crimson, he having made a great name for himself in the coaching world of other institutions, namely Amherst, his previous employment." The Manchester column by John C. "Finney" Burke that appeared in the March 31 issue of the *Beverly Evening Times*, noted: "John 'Stuffy' McInnis's Harvard nine will make their 1949 debut at the University of Virginia next Monday. It will be the first game for the Cambridge team under the helm of the famed Philadelphia A's first sacker, who resides on Tappan Street." Harvard sent its baseball team on the three-game tour to the warmer climate of the south before the home opener at Soldiers Field on April 12 against Boston University. The *Times* sports page reported on that same game April 4: "John 'Stuffy' McInnis, former big league great, will send his nine against the University of Virginia at Charlottesville this afternoon."

Even before Stuffy opened formal practice at Harvard, he took part in a clinic at Briggs Cage the first week in February, sponsored by the Boston Braves for "an assembled mob of high school coaches, H.A.A. moguls and passersby on the care and feeding of future stars," as the

Harvard Crimson put it. The featured speakers were slugger Earl Torgeson and pitcher Red Barrett of the Braves, and Harvard's new baseball coach. In a Feb. 7 *Crimson* column, "Egg In Your Beer, the Winter Circuit," student writer Donald Carswell had this to say:

> The extra added attraction of this particular Braves baseball clinic was the first local appearance of John P. McInnis, late of the Philadelphia Athletics, the Boston Red Sox, Norwich University and Amherst College. Stuffy McInnis gave the lecture on first base play.
>
> Stuffy is a smallish gray-haired man who played first base when Eddie Collins was at second, Jack Barry at short, and Home Run Baker was on third. He learned his baseball as part of the greatest infield of an era, and from the way he talked, it seemed he had learned it well. As part of his talk, McInnis demonstrated a foolproof method of running down erring base runners with just two pegs (throws). Nobody had ever seen it before, but this spring everybody who even sees the Sand Point Tigers play will see it.
>
> Above all, Stuffy McInnis emphasized that the secret of good defensive play is teamwork, and that the pivot of an infield is its first baseman. His part of the program was purely defensive baseball; McInnis' theories on how to hit a baseball will have to wait until he holds his first Harvard practice session in March."

Stuffy left the batting lecture to Torgeson, the Braves slugger.

Once practice was well under way, Stuffy held daily workouts for his squad all by himself, without an assistant coach or even a graduate volunteer. From the Harvard point of view, his official title was manager of the baseball team, not coach. In a way that was more appropriate, since baseball teams at the professional and even many amateur programs use the term manager. But at Harvard he was both manager and coach, with emphasis on the latter. Some of those who showed up at Briggs Cage in February were probably just curious and wanted to see what the famous new man was like. Others were seriously interested in baseball but lacked enough of a background to play at a college level. He had to whittle his squad of hopefuls down to a varsity size, and set up a junior varsity team, to keep some of the underclassmen and those who weren't quite good enough to make the top 18 or 20 involved, with an eye on the future. For those who really loved the game and wanted to play, Stuffy was anxious to keep them active. Meanwhile he had to get his best players ready for the three game southern road trip that would open the season. After what the *Crimson* described as a "generally unstable start," Stuffy's team pulled together and compiled a decent if unspectacular record of 10 wins and 12 losses in the Eastern Independent Baseball League, just a tad behind Dolph Stamborski's 12-11-1 slate of the year before. In games against Ivy League competition, the Crimson was 5-4. A highlight of the season occurred in late May when as a feature of "Old Home Week," when past graduating classes return for reunions, Amherst's baseball team, with Paul Eckley back on the bench, would travel to Cambridge. The *Crimson* headlined it "Strong Jeff Nine Visits Old Coach Today." The lead sentence: "Amherst, the team Stuffy McInnis did wonders for last spring, will try to beat its former coach this afternoon when it visits Soldiers Field for a 3:45 p.m. game." It was noted that the Lord Jeffs' starting lineup included six men who had played for Stuffy during the 10-1 '48 campaign. Now Amherst was 9-1, a scoring machine which in four of their wins had plated 12, 16, 16 and 22 base runners. The *Crimson* writer wasn't too confident about Harvard's chances that day, noting that the home team "seems headed in the right direction for the home stretch but is still somewhat unpredictable." But even if the team didn't win, Stuffy must have been delighted to see his old friends again. This was college baseball, not the professional wars, and he was, after all, an honorary member of the Amherst Class of 1948.

With his first season at Harvard in the books, from all evidence Stuffy did not spend the summer of 1949 relaxing at his Manchester home. Maybe he needed the money a summer job would provide, or maybe he was too much in love with baseball to stay away from the game until next February. His parents had come to Gloucester from Nova Scotia many years before, so he undoubtedly still had many contacts in the Canadian province. He'd head there for July and August. According to "Play Hard, Play Fast, Play Ball," a production of the Nova Scotia Sports Hall of Fame based in Halifax, Stuffy McInnis ("once a member of the Philadelphia Athletics famed $100,000 infield"), managed the Stellarton Albions of the Nova Scotia Baseball League for the '49 summer season "with nine imports." The term import meant players brought in from the United States.

In 1949, the Nova Scotia league, once mainly for "home grown" players, had assumed a new importance as a summer destination for U.S. collegians. In the years right after World War II, many college baseball players gravitated to the Northern League, an amateur summer circuit that operated in small cities in the three northern New England states. But in addition to helping players find part-time summer jobs, it appears that management of some of the teams also handed out small sums of "expense money." When that came to the attention of the Eastern Collegiate Athletic Conference, the ECAC declared in the fall of 1948 that the Northern was a "professional league." Any undergraduate collegian who played for a team in that circuit risked the loss of amateur status and continued eligibility to play college ball. Suddenly the Nova Scotia summer loop became a destination of choice, and many of the Northern League's former players chose Canada instead. That meant fewer openings for the natives as Americans took their spots. But although Stuffy's roster included nine "imports," he relied heavily on two Nova Scotians, Harry Reekie and John "Twit" Clarke, both of whom worked day jobs in the mines and emerged to play ball in the evening. The Nova Scotia Sports Hall of Fame was told by Clarke that Stuffy once said: "I can't figure out how they do it. They work all day in the mines, they come up here, they have a shower and maybe grab a sandwich, and they play ball, and they play good ball." The American lads might have a good thing going, but the Nova Scotians could not be faulted for their stamina or desire. Stuffy might have a story or two to tell any son of Harvard who complained about his workload. He wasn't the only American college coach to take a trip north, as Hank Swasey of the University of New Hampshire also managed for a time in Nova Scotia. It was strictly a one-year stint for Stuffy, as Johnny Watterson managed the Albions in 1950.

Back at Harvard for his second season, Stuffy found himself overwhelmed with eager ballplayers of varying skill levels when he issued his call for candidates as winter began to give way to spring. He had to deal with a turnout of 80 young men in 1950, all equipped with gloves and enthusiasm, some of whom with little else. Making cuts as gently as he could, he had managed after a month to whittle the squad down to 50, still an unworkable number for one man and one team. The *Crimson* reported on March 23 in a piece by reporter Herbert S. Meyers: "Briggs Cage has the atmosphere of a florist's greenhouse. The sun comes through a glass roof and mixes with the rising dust so that breathing becomes a very difficult chore. Oddly enough one man who spends a lot of time in the cage isn't even worried about breathing. Some sport they're playing there with bats and balls is enough to keep him fully occupied. Stuffy McInnis started spring baseball practice with some 80 men. He now has 50, and from 2 to 5 p.m. he holds practice without any help." Asked by Meyers during a rare break how the season shaped up, the coach kiddingly took refuge in talking about the Boston Red Sox upcoming campaign: "Well, if Doerr (Bobby) and Williams (Ted) get through without any injuries, and McDermott (meaning young pitcher Mickey) comes through ...... it's really too early to tell."

That could pretty much sum up Harvard's outlook with the opening contest of a 19-game schedule just three weeks away. Not only had Stuffy yet to decide on the 18 or 20 men who would make up the varsity, he also had to put together a JV team and another squad of freshmen, who at that time weren't eligible for varsity. He'd have to watch out for all of them over the spring season. Even among the more experienced players, position shifts were the order of the day. Walking around the fringes of the cage, reporter Meyers saw last year's outfielder Hal Moffie working out at second base, team captain John Caulfeld, normally a right fielder, learning first base, Cliff Crosby, usually a catcher, playing third, and about 15 men trying to impress the coach with their ability to pitch. Shortstop Johnny White appeared set, and another Harvard football player, Charlie Walsh, was making a bid to take the starting catcher position away from Crosby. All in all it was a work in progress. Not making things easier was the schedule, which showed 10 of the last 11 games away from Cambridge. Fortunately, most of the non-Ivy opponents were colleges in the greater Boston area.

Stuffy's one frustration stemmed from having to decide the final varsity spots. "The way it is now, I hate to cut anyone. Take that kid over there. Now suppose he's a late starter, say I keep him on (varsity), and one game comes and he pinch hits in the winning run. That would be swell, but how can I tell what he can do? It's pretty tough to work with 50 men all season, you know. If he had a chance to develop....." As it turned out, the Crimson finished the 1950 season with a very respectable 9-6 record (5-2 Ivy), with four of the originally scheduled 19 games cancelled, likely due to the uncertain weather of early spring. This time, when Harvard traveled to Amherst, the *Crimson* newspaper had a very different outlook, with a May 10 headline that read, "Varsity nine, behind Godin, plays weak Amherst club on road today." Unlike the Lord Jeffs' juggernaut of 1949, Eckley's club had been decimated by graduation and an injury to star pitcher Don Dunbar, causing the *Crimson* to brand the team "worst since the war." Stuffy, the paper said, "would really like to win this one." With Ira Godin taking the mound, Harvard's lineup, "unchanged from the one that stopped Navy here Saturday," had Cliff

Crosby catching, an infield from third to first of Myles Huntington, John White, Tom Cavanaugh and John Caulfeld, with Bernie Akillian, Ed Foynes and Hal Moffie patrolling the outfield. Godin, making his fourth start, was looking for his first victory.

After the 1950 success, Stuffy never enjoyed another winning season. Over the next four years his teams compiled a combined record of 28-44-1, for a six-year Harvard career mark of 47-62-1 (22-27 in Ivy play). One of the highlights of 1952 was the meeting between Harvard and Holy Cross on May 10, with the 5-0 Crusaders favored over the 3-4-1 Crimson. Stuffy chose to start promising right-handed sophomore John Arnold, who in his two appearances had pitched a complete game win over Yale and six innings of strong relief against B.U. But what made the day memorable was that the two opposing coaches were Stuffy and his old infield teammate with both the A's and Sox, Jack Barry, who had returned to coach his alma mater, the Crusaders. Stuffy and Jack loved to tease each other, and when they met at home plate to exchange lineup cards and go over the ground rules, their minds were far less on the game than in reliving a long-past error in a game in Boston, a rare miscue charged to Stuffy, but which the old first baseman always believed should have been given instead to his friend Barry for a low throw. The conversation was reported to have gone like this.

McInnis: "How are you, Jack?"

Barry: "I'm just fine, Stuffy. It's good to see you."

McInnis: "You know the throw was low, Jack!"

Stuffy's 7-13 Harvard team of 1954 was his last. He wasn't able to answer the bell in 1955. Now 64 years old, and suffering from the early symptoms of Parkinson's disease, his aging body no longer permitted him to coach with the energy he had always displayed. The years finally had taken their toll on "That's the Stuff, Kid." He resigned, and settled down in retirement at his Manchester home with his beloved Elsie for the years that remained to him.

THE MANCHESTER YEARS, ANOTHER RECORD, AND LAST INNING

"Stuffy was a very private person, he had a low key presence. But he had a striking appearance"

— John C. 'Finney' Burke, who remembers Stuffy well

I f Stuffy McInnis had wanted to be a celebrity resident of the pretty little seaside community of Manchester, the history of which dates back to 1645 when the tiny settlement village originally called Jeffrey's Creek was allowed to break free from the bounds of Salem to become a separate town, he certainly had every right to claim such a distinction. But that was not Stuffy's way. He never wanted the spotlight, never sought out the media, or chose to boast of his place in the annals of professional baseball. He'd submit to an interview on rare occasions if one was requested, but never initiated the contact, and even when with friends seems to have had little to say about his distinguished baseball career.

John C. "Finney" Burke remembers Stuffy well. A Manchester native and lifelong newspaperman, Burke began his career right out of high school in 1947 by covering his hometown for the *Beverly Evening Times*. After becoming managing editor of the Beverly paper, he joined the *Boston Globe* in 1964 to be assistant managing editor, and in retirement remained at age 79 a consultant for the Boston paper.

"Stuffy was a very private person, he had a low-key presence," Burke recalled. "But he had a striking appearance, with a button-down shirt and a tweed jacket. He was a very handsome man." For someone who had never been a scholar, Stuffy loved to read, said Burke, and could if he chose converse in a learned way on any number of subjects. But he seldom talked about his baseball career. Elsie McInnis also was recalled as "an impeccable dresser, very stylish."

Finney Burke got to know Stuffy at the former ballplayer's favorite hangout in Manchester, the back room of Brown's Market at the corner of Beach and Summer streets, almost next to the Manchester railroad station on the Gloucester Branch of what was then the Boston & Maine Railroad. Except for his own dwelling on Tappan Street, it was the place in town where he felt most at home. Stuffy would cross over a little wooden bridge that is gone now, then pass through the railroad yard where freight cars for the former Samuel Knight coal and lumber company were unloaded, to reach the back door of the market. Brown's was for many years a Manchester institution. It began as a fruit store operated by Greek immigrant Peter A. Brown, born Peter Tsalidas, who came to America with his brother Charles and settled in Manchester. He and his wife Anastasia had 10 children, and they became one of the leading business families in town.

His daughter Constance P. Brown, "Connie," told of how the family name was changed. "My father was sitting around with some friends, and one of them said, 'Now that you're in the USA, you need an American name. Nobody here can spell Tsalidas.' My father said, 'What do you suggest?' They read off a bunch of names, and he picked Brown." When the original fruit store became too small, the business was moved to the location near the tracks, popular grocery aisles were added, and it became Brown's Market. Generations of Manchester residents did their food shopping there. After many years, when the family decided it was time to retire, Brown's Market was sold to Jim Crosby, owner of a small chain of food stores with North Shore locations including Salem and Hamilton, so Crosby's Market carries on the Brown tradition. It was the Browns, and especially the Brown sons, who made Stuffy McInnis feel most at home.

"We always kept the back door unlocked for him," recalled Connie Brown. "We had a pot-bellied stove in the back room, so it was good and warm in the winter. Stuffy would sit in the back room and talk with my brothers, Paul and Spike and Teddy, sometimes George but he was younger. We girls would be out front working while the boys got to hang out in the back room." Ted Brown remembers Stuffy as "the nicest guy in the world." In addition to hanging out at the market with the baseball legend, Paul Brown, a future real estate man, and Spike, remembered for his radio play by play of high school and college football games, as boys delivered newspapers to Stuffy's home. Private though he was, Stuffy always had time for a short chat and a bit of advice whenever he met a child. "He loved talking to children," said Connie. When Stuffy drove, for many years he could be seen behind the wheel of a big Oldsmobile.

Manchester resident and former newspaper editor Gordon Abbott, in his book "Jeffrey's Creek," published in 2003 by the Manchester Historical Society, included an article on Stuffy. Wrote Abbott on page 271: "His daughter, Eileen Littlefield, remembers him as a kind and loving father who was understandably often away from home. Her mother, the former Elsie Dow of Manchester, held the household together when Stuffy traveled from city to city by train and Pullman car as everyone did in those days. 'He was wonderful with kids of every age,' she recalled, 'and made a lot of friends wherever he went. But he was basically a shy person. I don't think he ever really enjoyed the spotlight.'" Abbott also quoted from a 1949 story in the *Boston Herald* by William F. Homer, written when Stuffy began coaching at Harvard, in which the old ballplayer compared the current major league game with the rough-and-ready baseball of his day: "Baseball's different today. We hit against the spit ball, the shine ball and the emery" (in which pitchers scuffed the cover with an emery board kept in their waistband). "Pitchers would even use the ball to knock the mud off their spikes. We'd try to keep the old ball in play until it went out of the park. Now it's thrown out if it gets a hard look."

Stuffy kept up with local athletics at Manchester's high school, then called Story High. During his college coaching days he could seldom get to see the baseball team play. But in the 1940s and '50s, Story, lacking enough male students for a full football team, played a six-man version – two ends, a center, quarterback and two running backs -- a wide-open game in which everyone except the center was an eligible pass receiver. Hamilton, Rockport, Georgetown, Essex Aggie, Lancaster, Mass. and Eliot, Maine also fielded six-man teams back then, so there were enough for a league. Then there was basketball, which Stuffy followed avidly in the winter months when baseball was absent from the scene. Eileen McInnis and the girls team had to endure the frustrations of a rather gentle six-player contest back then in which only the forwards could shoot, dribbling was greatly restricted, and nobody could cross the center court line. The sport was more active for the boys, and Stuffy was one of the most faithful fans. Joseph Hyland, for whom the home field used by Manchester-Essex Regional High School teams is named, was the long-time sports coach at Story High. But for several weeks one basketball season, Stuffy stepped in to pinch hit for him. Finney Burke recalls that it was in the winter of 1945, when he was still in school. Joe Hyland came down with a case of mumps, then a common highly contagious childhood disease before vaccines were developed. Joe apparently had not been exposed as a child, and now he caught it, probably from a youngster in the school system. For an adult, a case of mumps could be an unpleasant experience. "Stuffy took over coaching the team and he did a very good job," said Burke. "He had a wonderful way of handling players. He was quick to praise, and he corrected mistakes in a pleasant way."

None of the biographical summaries for Stuffy make any mention of basketball, but there is one tantalizing clue that the great first baseman might not have been a stranger to playing the sport. A column published on July 17, 2007 written by Bill Kipouras, long-time sports writer for the *Salem News*, concluded with these words: "Part of the Stuffy McInnis legacy is that he also performed on the Original Celtics with Nat Holman." The Original Celtics, who had no connection with the Boston Celtics, were a barnstorming professional basketball team of the 1920s that took on all comers. Rosters don't seem to be available, but names associated with the team on web sites such as Wikipedia include Holman, "Dutch" Dehnert, Joe Lapchick, John Beckman, George "Horse" Haggerty and Davey Banks. At some point Stuffy, the consummate athlete, must have hooked up with them for a while. If so, he certainly had the credentials to fill in as a high school coach.

Stuffy undoubtedly watched some summer baseball in town. From 1947-1951 the Amaral-Bailey Post of the American Legion sponsored a men's team in the Senior Essex County Legion League. For several seasons Manchester and Beverly Farms played a best-of-seven season ending series, alternating games between Brook Street Playground in Manchester and Dix Park in Beverly Farms, to settle the "shoreline bragging rights." It was good baseball, well covered in the local press, that certainly must have attracted Stuffy's interest. After the Senior Legion teams folded, the Manchester Mariners entered the Intertown Twilight League with Rockport, Ipswich, Essex, Hamilton, Topsfield, Rowley, and, for a while, Beverly Farms. Little League Baseball came on the scene in 1952 when Manchester, Essex, Hamilton and Beverly Farms combined to form an Inter-Town league. Nobody remembers whether Stuffy attended any of the kids' games, but he might well have, thinking back on those boyhood days in Gloucester when he, his brothers and their friends played on March evenings under the streetlight with a knitted homemade ball.

But after his active baseball days ended in 1928, another sporting interest awaited Stuffy. That was golf, and being the splendidly conditioned athlete that he was, it wouldn't be long until he was making a name for himself on North Shore fairways. There would be no handicaps for him, and he became known as almost a "scratch" golfer who claimed once to have shot a 67 for 18 holes at Salem's private Kernwood Country Club. Stuffy enjoyed playing with friends at several area layouts, his favorite was the attractive public nine-hole, par 32 Candlewood Golf Course in Ipswich. To this day, Stuffy McInnis holds the course record at Candlewood, a gaudy 27, and that may be one record nobody will ever break.

Author Gary Larrabee wrote in the August-September 2009 issue of "North Shore Golf" magazine: "The oldest unmatched standard was set by the pride of Gloucester, former major leaguer John 'Stuffy' McInnis, who after a 19-year playing career.....retired with a .307 batting average and became a regular at Candlewood in Ipswich. In the 1930s McInnis shot 5 under par on the sporty Route 133 layout. No one has matched that number since." Bill Kipouras's July 17, 2007 column which appeared in both the *Salem News* and the *Gloucester Times*, was headed "Stuffy's golf mark still standing after all these years," and says the record round was shot in 1941. Kipouras interviewed Dave Whipple, director of operations at Candlewood, who said he was 6 years old that summer and his mother, Gladys, was running the course. He recalled Stuffy playing with and against some friends from Salem and described him as "a tough competitor. Kids were around to caddie for him but he always carried his own bag." Stuffy played Candlewood two or three times a week during the summer, and according to Whipple seldom talked baseball. "He was a wonderful guy. Stuffy was movie star handsome and friendly...... He was a humble man. He was not long (with his drives), but straight as an arrow on the golf course. He was accurate and could putt and chip."

Stuffy took special pride in his only child, Eileen, who inherited her mother's beauty. After graduating from Story High School, the popular Eileen matriculated at the two-year Endicott College in Beverly, where according to her lifelong best friend Mary Mahoney she was voted "Most Photogenic" in the Class of 1945. Endicott had been founded in the late

1930s by the husband and wife team of Charles O. Bierkoe as president and Eleanor Tupper as dean, on the expanded seaside campus of the former Kendall Hall School for girls. Originally a two-year junior college "of liberal arts and vocational arts for young women," it has now grown into a four-year coeducational institution, which also offers graduate degrees. Eileen married Charles Littlefield and they gave Stuffy and Elsie three grandchildren. The older son, John, died young, daughter Cynthia now lives in Maine, and the youngest, Richard, lives in the Magnolia section of Gloucester, a small part of which lies within the bounds of Manchester. The Littlefield family lived with Stuffy and Elsie in their later years and stayed on at Tappan Street after the McInnis's passing. For some time they owned the Village Hardware Store in Manchester and Eileen later worked for the Gillette Company. Richard Littlefield was only 4 years old at the time of his grandfather's death, so he retains few memories of Stuffy. One recollection that does remain is the big leather medicine ball, the type that used to be found in gymnasiums, which Stuffy kept in the back yard. "I remember my grandfather would tether me to it and we'd play," he said.

By the late 1950s, Stuffy's health was really starting to fail and he had to cut way back on his activities. There would be no more golf or anything else that took him far from home. Then in February of 1959 came the hardest blow he could receive, when his beloved Elsie passed away at age 67. "That really did him in," said "Finney" Burke. The gallant old pro survived his wife by just a year. Early in February of 1960, Stuffy suffered a fall at home, falls being a sometime consequence of Parkinson's disease, and severely injured a hip. For whatever reason, his physician had him transported not to Beverly Hospital or Addison Gilbert in Gloucester, but to Cable Memorial Hospital in Ipswich, a former small community hospital just a stone's throw from Stuffy's beloved Candlewood Golf Course. Perhaps he had lost his will to live or feared the consequences of being an invalid, but Stuffy failed to rally from the injury. On Feb. 16, 1960, he passed away, seven months short of his 70th birthday.

His death led the front page of the *Manchester Cricket* on Feb. 19. The headline read: "John P. 'Stuffy' McInnis, Baseball Immortal, Dies,' with a drop head "Lived in Manchester Over 40 Years." The writer of the story said he "was educated in the schools of Gloucester but left high school before graduation to carve out a career in baseball and to set marks as a major leaguer which have not to this day been equaled......" The story quoted Eddie Collins's remark about Stuffy wanting his infielders to make bad throws in order to give him practice, and added, "McInnis was grace personified as a first baseman despite the lack of height." And there was this tribute: "One of the greatest performances of his career came as it was ending. It was during the 1925 (world) series. He was inserted into the Pittsburgh lineup in the fifth game with Washington leading in the series three games to one.. Pittsburgh's morale was at a low point. McInnis proved a steadying influence on the club and it went on to sweep the next three games and win the world championship." The *Cricket* noted that Stuffy was survived by three of his four brothers, Albert of Philadelphia, William of Gloucester, and James of Woods Hole.

The headline in the *Beverly Evening Times* of Feb. 17 read: "Baseball World Mourns 'Stuffy' McInnis' Death." It was reported that he had been "in failing health for 3 years," and that 10 days before his passing he had fallen at home and broken a hip. The *Times* called Stuffy "One of baseball's greatest first basemen," and "One of the most highly respected men in sports." The writer, obviously unaware of the fact like nearly everyone at the time, did not mention Stuffy's Beverly connection and the fact that he was recommended to Connie Mack by Beverly's long forgotten Manager Madden. But undoubtedly prompted by Managing Editor Burke, the writer noted that Stuffy had followed home town sports "avidly," and "would often take a boy aside and give him advice which would later prove to have been exactly what the youngster needed to keep him from going the wrong way in life." The story also spoke of Stuffy's daily ritual in later years "of walking to Peter A. Brown's store to pick up the afternoon papers, where he always stopped to talk with sports-minded youngsters." Stuffy's death also made *The New York Times*, which carried a one column photo taken in later years beside the headline: "Stuffy M'Innis, 69; in $100,000 Infield." The *Times* noted that Stuffy had broken in with the Athletics as a shortstop in 1909 but became the team's regular first baseman two years later with Collins, Barry and Baker. "Connie Mack's fancy-fielding infield was known at the time as 'the $100,000 infield.' As prices and costs rose in later years, the tag seemed low. But half a century ago the group was higher-priced than any."

Following a wake at the Lee & Moody Funeral Home in Beverly, Stuffy's funeral Mass was celebrated on February 19 at Sacred Heart Church in Manchester, the Roman Catholic parish where he and Elsie had worshiped, with the Rev. John Connell officiating. Burial was in Manchester's Rosedale Cemetery. In a story the next day, the *Beverly Evening Times* reported that among the mourners at the service were two of Stuffy's former Red Sox teammates, Larry Woodall and Fred Maguire, and ex-New York Yankee "Jumping" Joe Duggan. Undoubtedly many other friends from the baseball world had preceded Stuffy to the other side, and others were either too frail or lived too far away to make the journey. But the church must have been filled with those who just remembered Stuffy McInnis as a modest man and a good neighbor.

Some 33 years after Stuffy left this world, there was a follow-up story involving his daughter Eileen. In 1993, the Boston Red Sox held a ceremony at Fenway Park to mark the 75th anniversary of the team's last World Series triumph in 1918. Four times in those 75 years – in 1946, 1967, 1975 and 1986 – the Sox made it to the World Series, only to lose the championship in seven games, to the Cardinals in 1946 and 1967, the Reds in 1975, and most hurtful of all, the Mets in 1986. There was even talk of a curse that Babe Ruth supposedly placed on his old ball club after he was sold to the Yankees. (That supposed "curse" was put to rest when the Sox took the World Series in 2004 and again in 2007.) Now in '93, surviving relatives of the 1918 players were invited to attend the ceremony, among them Ruth's daughter, and Eileen Littlefield, daughter of the peerless first baseman of the 1918 world champions. Mary Mahoney, Eileen's lifelong best friend, accompanied her to the ballpark that day. She remembers Eileen being given a souvenir scrapbook with mementoes of the World Series and the 75th anniversary, and a plaque. "She loved that day," Richard Littlefield said of his mother. But there was more. It may be recalled that the players in 1918 were ready to boycott the fifth game of the series because of their dissatisfaction with the money they were going to earn. The winning shares barely topped $1,100. Someone from the Red Sox front office researched the matter, and discovered that the players indeed had been shortchanged, to the tune of $250. For the relatives, it was decided to make good on the deficit, minus interest, of course. Envelopes with checks were passed out, with one going to Eileen McInnis Littlefield. Mary Mahoney remembers: "Eileen pointed at the sky, and said, 'Thanks, Dad!'" Stuffy McInnis was still taking care of his little girl.

Eileen, who lived in Magnolia, died at home on March 28, 2009. Her brief obituary published in the *Gloucester Times* on April 4 said she was born in Manchester-by-the-Sea, but did not include her parents' names. At her request, the funeral was private.

A SNUB FROM THE HALL OF FAME?

'Do I think Stuffy McInnis should adorn a plaque in Cooperstown? I sure do "
  – Will Anderson, 'The Lost New England Nine'

O n the face of it, Stuffy McInnis put up numbers that qualify him for inclusion among the baseball immortals enshrined in the National Baseball Hall of Fame and Museum in Cooperstown, N.Y., the place where baseball was NOT "invented." If one discounts his rookie season in 1909 when he mostly sat on the bench as an 18-year-old utility infielder, along with his final entry in 1927, when he made one token game appearance while managing the Phillies, "That's the Stuff" performed remarkably over a 17-year career, 14 seasons as an every day player. Once he settled in at first base in 1911, he played only that position, except for 23 games in 1918 when he bailed the Red Sox out of a jam by filling in capably at third base. His lifetime achievements on the baseball field are little short of amazing.

Consider:

Stuffy had a career batting average of .307 – some writers, apparently using a round-off system, have made it .308. He was one of the most consistent hitters the game ever saw, 12 times topping the benchmark for excellence of .300, including six years in a row from 1910-1915. Four other times he was just under that, hitting over .290. In his only "bad" offensive season if you could call it that, his .272 average in the Red Sox pennant winning year of 1918 when the entire team hit just .249, it has been pointed out Stuffy that year was suffering from boils which could have hindered his batting grip. Over the course of his career he played in 2,128 games, ranking him number 159 on the all-time major league list. In 7,822 official times at bat, he banged out 2,405 hits, putting him at number 113 all-time (statistics provided by *The Baseball Nexus*). He drove in 1,063 runs (101 in 1912) putting him at number 221, scored 872 runs and stole 172 bases. Two of his most amazing statistics involved "sacrifice hits" and strikeouts. On 383 occasions, Stuffy gave up his time at bat to bunt a teammate on the bases into scoring position. (Sacrifice flies were not a stat in his time.) Only two men in the history of the game have been credited with more sacrifice hits than Stuffy.

He also was one of the hardest men ever to strike out. Over his entire career, pitchers succeeded in fanning Stuffy only 189 times, whether swinging or being called out on strikes by the umpire, and his amazing batting eye got better as the years went by. (Strikeout totals were not recorded until 1912.) With the Red Sox in 1921 he fanned only 9 times, with Cleveland in 1922 just 5, with the Braves in 1924 just 6, and as a part-time player for the marvelous 1925 Pirates, only once in 155 at bats. If we carry that statistic a bit further and add on his 380 bases on balls, his 383 sacrifice bunts and the 59 times he reached base when hit by a pitch (none of which are included as official times at bat), Stuffy went to the plate 8,623 times. That means he struck out just once in every 45.6 times in the batter's box, which in today's game would be considered an impossibility. Figuring an average of four at-bats per game, pitchers got Stuffy out on strikes just once every 11 baseball contests. Talk about a contact hitter -- the little Gloucester native wrote the book on that skill. Of course batters in his time didn't have to face the modern day flamethrowers who fling the ball the 60 feet six inches between the mound and home plate at 95 miles per hour or better. But in other ways things were much tougher on hitters back then. As Stuffy himself said, the rules favored the pitchers. Deliveries that have been illegal for many years were allowed in the first two decades of the 20th century. Pitchers could load the baseball with saliva, including spitting tobacco juice on it. Even after the spitball was outlawed in the early 1920s, old timers such as Burleigh Grimes who had made their living using it for years were "grandfathered" to continue wetting up the occasional pitch without penalty. The "shine" ball was thrown by employing talcum powder.

Hurlers could scuff the ball with an emery board, slice the cover with their belt buckle or a sharp thumbnail to make the ball do tricks. As Stuffy recalled, on a wet field the pitcher might use the ball to knock the mud out of his spikes, then serve it up to the batter covered with slime. The poor catcher must not always have known what to expect, and by the third inning his mitt might be slippery with tobacco juice. In those days a baseball remained in use until it was knocked out of the playing area, so pitchers tried to hang onto a doctored ball for as long as possible. A foul ball that didn't reach the stands would quickly be chased down by a fielder and thrown back to his pitcher. As Stuffy said, a ball that hung around for a while was about as easy to hit for any real distance as a lump of coal, and on a dark, cloudy day might become so soiled that it was nearly impossible to see. Today, a baseball that acquires even a small scuff mark is thrown out of play by the umpire, and a new ball may be gone after just one pitch. No matter what they threw to Stuffy McInnis, it almost inevitably made contact with his bat.

Then there was Stuffy's remarkable fielding record with that little round glove. He said in later years that he made up for his lack of height as a first baseman by developing enough spring in his legs to leap for a high throw that normally could have been reached only by a much taller man. As Jasper Davis advised Connie Mack back in 1911, Stuffy would reach any high throw that any other first baseman could catch. Over the 1,995 games in which he appeared on defense for his five major league clubs (plus one brief appearance while managing the Phillies), Stuffy handled 19,962 putouts and 1,238 assists while being charged with only 160 errors, for a gaudy lifetime fielding percentage of .993 His record of 119 consecutive games a first base without an error stood until 2007, when it was broken by Kevin Youkilis of the Boston Red Sox. His 1,700 consecutive fielding chances without a miscue, set over two seasons, also was topped by Youkilis. Of his contemporaries, only Frank Chance and George Sisler might have rivaled him at first base. John Phelan McInnis had all the stuff as a major league baseball player.

Yet his name was all but forgotten until it came up over the airwaves and in print when Youkilis was closing in on his record. And despite his Hall of Fame statistics compiled long before the idea of an "all-star" game had been dreamed up, the sportswriters who vote for candidates to the shrine at Cooperstown ignored Stuffy. When the first Hall balloting took place in 1939, only four votes went Stuffy's way. The most votes he ever got came in 1949, a total of eight, or 5.2 percent of those cast. By then he had been gone from the game for more than two decades, so it's likely that very few of the writers had seen him play, and of those probably none when he was in the prime of his career, 1911-1922. Maybe he lacked the charisma of the game's more colorful characters, although that should have been no barrier when his record was considered. And if anyone had taken the time to look up the larcenous inside-the-park warmup pitch home run he perpetrated on the Red Sox in 1911, the only time in the history of the sport that anyone successfully "stole" three bases and home plate in one at-bat, they would have to agree that was as colorful a feat as the most discriminating baseball buff could ask for. There seem to be only two possible knocks on Stuffy McInnis that it could be argued disqualified him from the Hall of Fame. One, of course, is his lack of home run power. He hit only 20 round trippers in his long career, some of them inside the park such as the one just referred to. Power was not the little guy's game. Of his 2,405 regular season hits, all but 433 were singles. But it's the Baseball Hall of Fame, not the Sluggers Hall of Fame. Stuffy, with his on-base percentage of .343, his minuscule number of strikeouts and his consistent heads-up play was designed to help his team win baseball games. And while he played on four last-place clubs over the years, he also performed for six pennant winners. That's more than a lot of Hall of Famers can boast. And it could be argued that he deserved consideration if nothing else than for his incredible defensive play. The other argument might center around his poor hitting performance in baseball's World Series. It's true that in four trips to the fall classic (not including his token appearance in 1911 when the wrist injury kept him off the field), Stuffy went 13 for 65 at the plate, a .200 overall average. His first two appearances, in 1913 and 1914, produced a rather pathetic 4 hits in 31 at-bats. But when you combine his performances for Boston in 1918 and Pittsburgh in 1925, he went 9 for 34. Some of his hits for the Red Sox were crucial to their triumph, and his entry into the Pirates' lineup was instrumental in that team's rebound from a 1-3 deficit to win the World Series. As for that .200 average, the man who is arguably the greatest hitter of all time, the last man to top .400, war hero and slugger par-excellence Ted Williams of the Red Sox, only once in his great career made it to the World Series. That was in 1946, when the great Williams went 5 for 25 over the seven games, for a career World Series batting average of .200. But maybe it should be held against Stuffy by the purists. No longer eligible of course for Hall of Fame balloting, Stuffy's only hope would be the Veterans Committee, but that body only rarely puts forward the name of someone overlooked earlier.

Over the years a number of New Englanders have come forward to argue Stuffy's cause and lament how he has been so badly overlooked. One is Will Anderson, author of "The Lost New England Nine – The Best of New England's Forgotten Ballplayers." Anderson made McInnis the showpiece of his 2003 book, writing that Stuffy "should not be in this book simply because Stuffy McInnis should be in the Hall of Fame." (A typographical error in the chapter headline, repeated at least once in the copy before being corrected, spells the name "McGinnis.") Later on page 27 Anderson added: "Do I think Stuffy McInnis should adorn a plaque in Cooperstown? I sure do. Here is a player who is .308 lifetime over 19 seasons; ranks in the top 15 in six lifetime fielding categories; batted over .300 an even dozen times; rarely struck out; and played on six pennant winners and in five World Series. Legendary sportswriter Grantland Rice called Stuffy 'a wargod of the diamond.' My favorite sportswriter quote, though, comes from the typewriter of longtime Philadelphia scribe Wallace McCurley. Wrote Mr. McCurley: 'Where is the old Athletics fan who does not remember how, on a dark day, all one could see of a bad throw to McInnis was a spurt of dust in front of the bag? That was all – the ball then would be nestled in his glove.'"

Bob Ryan, a respected sports journalist, wrote a column for the *Boston Globe* on July 23, 1991 headed "Twelve Errors of Omission." Ryan said his original intention was to campaign for five former ballplayers he believed were entitled to admission to the Hall of Fame, but after a lot of research concluded there were more than that. Writing of Stuffy McInnis, Ryan noted that he was a "career .308 batter who K'd a scant 189 times in 7822 at bats." The fact that Stuffy does not have a plaque in Cooperstown, was, in Ryan's words, "absolutely a ridiculous exclusion."

Journalist/columnist Jeremiah V. Murphy, who grew up in Beverly and later lived in Rockport, took up Stuffy's cause in a *Boston Globe* column published on Jan. 31, 1993. Wrote the one-time Beverly athlete: "I have to tell you right up front that I'm not much of a big-league baseball fan any more. But I can't resist the temptation to write about the late Stuffy McInnis of Gloucester and Manchester-by-the-Sea. I think he got shafted by circumstances, because he never did make it into the Baseball Hall of Fame. He should be in there. No question about that."

Gordon Abbott, in "Jeffrey's Creek," quoted from a story by one-time Boston sportswriter Jack Denty: "It was a grave injustice that Stuffy McInnis passed away without being welcomed into the Hall of Fame..... Maybe he was punished for his lack of color. One thing for sure, he was not judged fairly on his record."

Another who has plugged for Stuffy is Melvin George of Rockport. When Youkilis broke the record for consecutive games without an error, the *Gloucester Daily Times* on June 26, 2007 published an article by correspondent Nate Rice, who interviewed George. The Rockport resident argued that when Stuffy played, he had to be on the field for all nine innings to get credit toward the record. But under modern rules, Youkilis could go into the game as a late inning replacement, as he did for David Ortiz in an inter-league contest at San Diego, and receive credit toward the errorless game record. George, wrote Rice, "has campaigned to no avail to get 'Stuffy' into the Baseball Hall of Fame."

Rice also interviewed Will Anderson, who told the writer he believed Stuffy would have received more Hall of Fame consideration had he played for a team such as the Yankees, Giants or Cardinals. The author of "The Lost New England Nine" said Stuffy's records are all the more significant because they were achieved with primitive equipment. The first baseman's glove, he noted was "something you might make a snowball with, but it's nothing you use to play first base. It was his artistry that made it, not the glove."

As for Stuffy, he undoubtedly would consider the argument not worth the fuss. He gave his best to the game of baseball and his best to leading a good life as a citizen, husband, father, coach and being a role model for youngsters. Glory was not his goal. But when all is said and done, questions rise like ghosts from long-forgotten baseball fields. What if Dick Madden had not invited a 16-year-old boy from Gloucester to join his Beverly baseball team in 1907? What if Stuffy had been too nervous to show his stuff against older men and the critical fans who filled the grandstand and lined the base paths at Peabody's Field? What if Dick Madden had not known Connie Mack, and what if Mack had not trusted Madden's opinion that a small 17-year-old kid was ready to help a big league ball club? And what if Mack had lost confidence in the kid after he made 10 errors in 14 games as a fill-in rookie shortstop, and the fans must have been yelling at him to get that kid out of there, and he had bought Stuffy a train ticket back to Boston? Would he have lived his life as an anonymous worker for some firm in Gloucester and an occasional player for another semi-pro club? But those things didn't happen. John Phalen McInnis proved over and over again that he had the stuff, all right.

APPENDIX 'A' -- PEABODY'S FIELD – BEVERLY'S LOST TREASURE

"Of all the sad words of tongue or pen
The saddest are these: it might have been."
   – John Greenleaf Whittier, "Maud Muller"

You won't find Peabody's Field on any modern day map of Beverly, nor will you find a sign, plaque or any other clue to mark the place where enthusiastic crowds gathered to watch baseball games in the early years of the 20th century. That forgotten location was where Stuffy McInnis made a name for himself in the 15 months between the time he joined Dick Madden's team as a skinny little 16-year-old high school boy from Gloucester, and the time Madden recommended him to Connie Mack as a sure-fire future major league ballplayer. Stuffy proved that Madden, whose duties with the Submarine Signal Company took him across the Atlantic to London, could not be faulted as a judge of baseball talent, and Mack must many times have been glad he listened to the advice of the Beverly manager. Even "Doc" Martin, the other player Mack signed at the same time as Stuffy on Madden's recommendation, made it to the "big time" with the Athletics, if only for 14 games. It would be nice to know how Madden became friendly with the legendary Mack.

While Peabody's Field was for about a decade Beverly's most important baseball facility, it never belonged to the city. It was owned by the Prospect Hill Realty Trust, whose trustee and principal owner was Henry W. Peabody, who divided his time between Salem and Beverly and was a leading citizen of both communities. His estate in Beverly was "Parramatta" at 70 Corning Street, which in 1911-12 his widow made available to President William Howard Taft and his family. Peabody also controlled the Montserrat Syndicate and other real estate trusts. He had developed housing on Prospect Hill and on the southerly side of Essex Street, but the large tract bordered on the south by Essex Street, on the north by Odell Avenue, on the east by Spring Street and on the west by Baker Avenue remained open space. The steam trains of the Boston & Maine's Gloucester Branch passed right by the facility. It was a swing of the bat away from the Montserrat depot, which Mr. Peabody named for his favorite island in the West Indies. At that time it was a sleepy flag stop (as shown by a 1906 timetable), patronized by residents of the outer Cove neighborhood and the then very sparsely populated Centerville, with no freight house. In a generous civic gesture, Mr. Peabody allowed the city of Beverly to use his property as a baseball park, which was informally known by his last name. In addition to Madden's solidly supported semi-pro team, the Beverly High School nine used the field, as did the baseball team sponsored by the United Shoe Machinery Corp., which after its establishment in Beverly by 1905 went out of its way to provide numerous athletic opportunities for its employees and their families.

As has been pointed out, no photographic evidence of Peabody's Field exists in the collection of the Beverly Historical Society. There is a photo of a Beverly men's baseball team from the early 20th century, which unfortunately lacks even a shred of information or an accession number to give a clue as to its origin. It could be Madden's team, which seems to have been the only team of its type in those years. Near the end of the second row is a lad who appears to be the youngest player and who might (or might not) be Stuffy McInnis. The 1907 Beverly Assessors map book at the Historical Society shows a 13-acre open tract, but which contains a structure labeled "grand stand." Madden's team sold reserved seating in that grandstand, and accounts also mention bleachers for seating, which might have been more of a temporary seasonal nature. As many as 1,000 spectators could be comfortably accommodated, and advertisements for the Beverly team in the local paper reveal it cost a quarter to gain admission. From this information it is clear that a lot of work went into making Peabody's Field a first-class baseball facility that could attract quality out-of-town opposition for Madden's men, and it was not intended to be just a stop-gap accommodation. Furthermore, it is obvious that Henry Peabody did not look at the property as a future site to make more money on housing; instead, he desired that the city acquire permanent possession of his land for continued use as a ball field.

This became clear in 1907, the year Stuffy McInnis showed up. In their annual report for 1906, Beverly's Park Commissioners, Joseph W. Preston, John H. Harris and Edmund Putnam, included a recommendation that "under the Play-Ground Act, the lot between Essex Street and the Boston & Maine Railroad tracks, known as Peabody's field" be acquired by the city. The Play-Ground Act passed by the Massachusetts Legislature not long before, allowed municipalities to purchase land for playground purposes, either through negotiation or by an eminent domain taking. Things decidedly heated up in '07. The *Beverly Evening Times* informed its readers on May 10 that Henry Peabody had offered to sell the entire parcel to the city for $26,500 (a figure later reduced by $500). This was considered by some people to be a bargain. The *Times* on June 6 headlined a story: "Every Reason for Taking the Land." It quoted Park Commissioner Putnam, who "tells us as a citizen why Beverly should secure Peabody's Field. The price is low, location is good, taxpayers and summer residents favor it." At the same time, Beverly High School (BHS) students up the road at 3 Essex Street held an "enthusiastic mass meeting" at which they endorsed city acquisition of Peabody's Field. The BHS student body enjoyed having their baseball team play at such a convenient location, and also liked to be able to watch the semi-pro games. Earlier, on May 11, the *Saturday Evening Citizen* reported on a meeting of the Common Council the previous Thursday, at which, "Among the new orders was one for the purchase of Peabody field for a playground. The owner offers the land from Spring st. to Sargent av. for $26,000. This is about 21/2 cents per foot." A subcommittee of councilmen McCarthy, Torrey and Trask was appointed to consider the matter. In those days Beverly had two legislative bodies. In addition to the Board of Aldermen there was a lower branch called the Common Council; together they were referred to as the City Council. Perhaps adding an ominous note, the same issue told that "Mayor Dow and the heads of the city departments held a conference Monday night with a view to cooperate to keep down the city expenses." S. Harvey Dow, obviously, had run for mayor on an austerity plank.

Next, a Citizens Planning Committee was organized in an effort to get the public behind the proposal. On Aug. 1, the *Times* reported that the committee had been busy putting together a schematic designed to do just that. The line drawing published along with the story showed that in addition to the main baseball diamond where the "big" teams played, there would be a "boys ball field," a football field, tennis courts, a quarter mile cinder running track around the perimeter, a manicured croquet lawn, a shaded pavilion where elders could sit in comfort out of the sun, and even a camping area "for small boys where they can have fun tenting without being too far from home." The new and improved Peabody's Field, in other words, would have something for all ages and interests, and would be a showplace recreational facility not only for Beverly but outstripping almost anything else available on the North Shore. Apparently with some donated funds, the Citizens Planning Committee printed 5,000 placards detailing the proposal, which were to be distributed to every household and business establishment in Beverly.

But not everybody thought it was such a great idea. One doubter was the editor of the *Saturday Morning Citizen*, who was skeptical at best, perhaps wishing to take the opposite side of the issue from that promoted by the daily paper. In the June 1 paper, under a headline "The Only Way," he wrote: "We cannot see how the Mayor can consistently sign an order for the purchase of Peabody field, even if such an order should pass, as he has set up as an apostle of economy. There is considerable question about such an order passing both branches...... The only way in which the Peabody field order can hope for the Mayor's signature is in the nature of a referendum and this matter could be voted on by the people at the next municipal election. There really isn't any hurry. A referendum order should satisfy all parties and if the people really want the field they can say so; after all it is the only way to settle a vexed question."

On Aug. 3, after the Citizens Planning Committee distributed its explanatory placards to one and all, the Citizen expounded: "If any citizen is not familiar with Peabody field it will not be the fault of the committee. 5,000 cards giving a map and description of the proposed playground have been distributed. We printed this last week." (A glance at the previous week's paper did not show this.)

"While it is improbable that either branch of the City Council will pass an order for purchase this year, or that the mayor would sign such an order, the committee believe that a campaign of education will pave the way for a purchase next year."

Ah yes, next year; there was always next year. But after the initial burst of enthusiasm and the efforts of the citizens committee, the matter of acquiring Peabody's Field seems to have been shoved to the municipal back burner. There is no evidence that much of any consideration was paid to the matter by the city government in 1908. No effort was proposed to put the question before the voters through a referendum. In the words of the late Boston Celtics broadcaster Johnny Most, the city fathers "fiddled and diddled," without ever taking a stand to "stop and pop." After all, the *Saturday Morning Citizen* had advised, "There really isn't any hurry." Peabody's Field was there, and it was unlikely that its owner would make any move to take it away. But 1908 flew by on its course, and next year never came. On Dec. 7, 1908, Henry W. Peabody passed away at the age of 70. At the end of his lengthy obituary, the *Citizen* noted: "It was through his generosity that the Peabody field was used as a playground for so many years, and it was his desire that this plot should be taken by the city."

It was too late, much too late. The successor trustees to the real estate syndicate had no interest in seeing the parcel continue to be a ballfield, not when there was considerable money to be made by building houses there. Although the trust supposedly gave the city until March 1 to complete acquisition, well before the winter was over there were surveyors roaming all over the former ball park, staking out five streets between Essex and Odell which would be given the names of Hawthorne, Magnolia, Lowell, Sherman and Bertram. The Park Commissioners had already yielded up the cause for lost, writing in their annual report for the City Documents on Jan. 25, 1909: "It is much to be regretted that the so-called 'Peabody's Field' has been lost to the city. It has been recommended by this Board time and again as a suitable inland playground and should in justice to posterity have been purchased." The report was signed by commissioners Preston, Harris and Putnam who lamented, presumably along with the Citizens Planning Committee which worked so hard on the blueprint, and many other residents, that the city government had so badly dropped the ball by letting a vital municipal asset get away when it could have been purchased inexpensively.

Before spring, steam powered equipment had bulldozed the grandstand, backstop and fencing, and was grading the site of what had been proposed as a magnificent public park. The streets and about 80 single-family house lots were being staked out. Edward T. Harrington, the sales agent for the Prospect Hill Syndicate, set up an office at 157 Essex Street, with a telephone line, Beverly 721, and launched his marketing campaign the same week in which Madden's team had opened the baseball season the year before. An advertisement in the *Beverly Evening Times* on April 17, 1909 touted the future of Peabody's Field: "Let us sell you a lot on this desirable property on Patriots Day.... Buy before the price goes up." Harrington expounded on the proximity of the Montserrat station, which that year was to shake off its back country flag stop status and take on a new importance with the exciting announcement that President Taft was making Beverly his summer capital. He and his family were going to spend the season at the Stetson "Cottage" (actually a substantial structure) on the grounds of the Robert and Maria Antoinette Evans waterfront estate off Ober Street, which we now know as Lynch Park. Taft and his retinue or aides and reporters were to bring their special trains to a siding at Montserrat. This, noted Harrington, would make owning a home in his development all the more prestigious. By 1911, many of the new homes on the five streets had been built and were occupied. Now there were streets and back yards where Stuffy and his teammates had run down baseballs while hundreds cheered them on.

The negative impact on baseball in Beverly was sudden and dramatic. We don't know whether Dick Madden, having completed his voyage abroad for his employers at Submarine Signal Company, was prepared to put his team on the field again in 1909. (The record has him living in Beverly until 1915, when he had sailed away to the London office.) But if he was thinking of local baseball again, it couldn't happen because there was no home stadium where the semi-pro club could play. Beverly fans could no longer turn out with their quarters for admission to watch the locals take on Rockport, Wakefield, Somerville, Marlboro and the other top clubs in the state. They wouldn't be climbing aboard trains to follow their favorites to games out of town. Semi-pro ball wasn't the only program to take a hit from the demise of Peabody's Field. Despite enthusiasm for sports on the part of Principal B. Sumner Hurd and Superintendent Adelbert Safford, Beverly High School wouldn't field a baseball team in the spring of 1909. With no suitably equipped public baseball facility within safe walking distance of the high school, the season was canceled, much to the disappointment of young students who had eagerly awaited their chance to take the field for the Orange and

Black. Organized baseball in Beverly was kept alive that year only by the Sunday School League. That circuit played its games at the only other real ballpark in the city, Lovett's Field in North Beverly, located close to the site of today's Henry's Market. The First Baptist, Dane Street, North Beverly and Universalist churches all sponsored teams, with a fifth entry coming from Wenham and a sixth varying from year to year. The name sounds very genteel, but the Sunday School League was a hotly competitive circuit that charged ten cents admission per game (ladies free), and despite its far from central playing location seems to have drawn fans who could get their baseball fix nowhere else. The teams were made up of older youths and young men, not Sunday school children. Games were known to become rowdy, spiced with loud arguments and near fights. Finally, the league's directors moved to rein in the un-Christian rowdyism by hiring a tough, no nonsense, hard-fisted umpire who was given a mandate to restore order. He seems to have been successful. The Beverly Historical Society owns a photo of the North Beverly Sunday School League team. Beverly High School resumed baseball in 1910, traveling to Lovett's Field for games.

Faced with a crisis due to a lack of centrally located adequate playing fields for baseball enthusiasts, the Park Commissioners needed a plan. They came up with a successful proposal to utilize land off Cedar Street, once part of the city's Poor Farm, but now no longer needed for agricultural purposes. By 1912, a new playing facility originally called the High School Athletic Field and later renamed Cooney Field, was being made ready for use, and Beverly once again had a proper baseball park. In addition to providing a new venue for baseball games, the facility was converted in the fall to a football field for the high school team, and a quarter-mile track also was installed. A photo from 1914 shows that the concrete spectator stands at the field were in place from the beginning. Before 1909, BHS home football games were played on the Beverly Common, which also had been used for baseball dating back to 1860. After the Beverly-Salem Thanksgiving morning football tradition took root, Salem objected to playing on the Common, citing unsafe field conditions. After agreeing to play two years in a row at Salem, BHS balked at doing so again in 1909. Salem refused to come to Beverly for a Thanksgiving tilt that year, forcing Beverly to set up a game with a Boston school on the holiday. Ironically, they didn't play on the Common. With a resident of nearby Dane Street seriously ill and needing quiet, the team moved all activities to Lovett's Field, where games were played for three seasons with players repairing at halftime to the nearby

North Beverly Fire Station. Once Cooney Field was ready, it became the home football venue until 1937, when the adjoining Hurd Stadium was built as a Depression-era Works Progress Administration project. Beverly baseball teams now had a proper spring and summer home once more, Babe Ruth hit his home run there in 1919, and Beverly soon had enough men's teams to launch its own twi-light league by the early 1920s.

At the request of Earle T. Wardell Post of the American Legion, the Athletic Field was renamed in 1921 for Robert James Cooney, one of the first Beverly natives killed in action in France during World War I. Cooney, who while a student lived at 13 Lovett St., was a member of the Beverly High School Class of 1910, a popular, talented athlete who was captain and right tackle for the 7-2-2 1909 football team as well as starting catcher on the 1910 baseball team that played at Lovett's Field. The "class prophesy" written by Marion Putnam for the June 1910 issue of the BHS *Aegis* literary magazine predicted that Bob Cooney would become "football coach for the Harvard Varsity team." According to the directory he moved to Seattle in 1912. Field lighting was installed at Cooney in the 1970s, but proved too dim for night baseball until the Beverly Babe Ruth League paid to greatly improve the lights early in the 21st century. Now with Cooney Field in top condition again and two first-class 60-foot fields lighted by the Beverly Little League on Harry Ball Park at 410 Essex Street, local baseball, including night baseball, is alive and well. One can only speculate on what things would look like today if the city had acquired Peabody's Field, followed through on the citizen committee's multi-use proposals, and kept it up with more improvements over the years. It might still be a recreational showplace today. On the other hand, the residents of five Montserrat neighborhood streets would have needed to find another address, and the city would have lost out on the property tax revenue from all those homes.

APPENDIX 'B' -- CONNIE MACK, A BASEBALL 'LIFER'

"No matter what I talk about, I always get back to baseball."
    – Connie Mack in 1951, at age 88

The man who signed Stuffy McInnis, kept him on the big league club despite some shaky play at shortstop as an 18-year-old rookie substitute, made him a part of the famous "$100,000 Infield," and saw him become one of the best first basemen ever to play the game, had many distinctions in the world of baseball. Unlike Stuffy, Connie Mack does have a plaque in the Hall of Fame, being a member of the Hall's original class for his many contributions to the sport, even though his own playing career was mediocre.

Mack was born to Irish immigrants in the middle of the Civil War, on Dec. 22, 1862 in the little central Massachusetts town of East Brookfield, near Spencer, southwest of Worcester. His birth name was Cornelius McGillicuddy, and although he went almost all his life by the shortened name of Mack, he never officially changed it. Forced to drop out of school at 14 when his ailing war veteran father could no longer support the family, young Connie went to work but soon realized that what he really wanted to do in life was play baseball. Starting with the East Brookfield semi-pro team, he moved on by the 1880s to play minor professional ball in the Connecticut League. He could play any position other than pitcher, but was best known as a catcher even though he threw left-handed. He made it to the majors in 1886 at 23, when he was signed by the Washington Nationals, for whom he played four seasons. In 1887 he married the "sunny and vivacious" Margaret Hogan of Spencer, who gave him three children before dying in 1892 from complications of her third childbirth. In 1890, Mack was one of the players who challenged baseball's "reserve clause" and the supremacy of the National League by forming the rival Players League. Connie put his money where his heart was, investing his $500 savings in the Buffalo club, and losing his cash when the Players League folded after just one season. Welcomed back to the majors with the Pittsburgh Pirates in 1891, he became the team's player-manager in 1894. In 11 seasons as a player he batted .245, but was known as a canny and smart catcher. He learned to make a clicking noise that sounded uncannily like a baseball tipping a bat. He'd do it when a hitter ducked out of the way of a high inside pitch, often fooling the umpire into calling the pitch a foul strike instead of a ball.

Retiring as a player after 1896, Mack was named manager of the Milwaukee Brewers in the Western League, a minor league that was run by Ban Johnson. As part of his salary he accepted a 25 percent share of the club, making him an owner for the first time. Johnson decided in 1901 to challenge the supremacy of the National League by changing the name of his circuit to the American League, putting teams in big cities and declaring major league status. One of the new teams was the Philadelphia Athletics, whose manager, treasurer and co-owner in partnership with Ben Shibe, was Connie Mack. Over the years he acquired majority ownership, although he did not become sole owner until 1936, and he compiled a record that nobody will ever approach by managing the Athletics for 50 seasons. Never wearing a uniform after he retired as a player, Mack managed with scorecard in hand, waving it to move his players around to play deeper, shallower or more toward the foul line, depending on who was at bat. (When the opposition caught on to his hand signals, he used the scorecard as a decoy.) Nothing got by him on the playing field, and writers began to refer to him in print as "the Tall Tactician." As has been pointed out, he was a man who didn't drink, didn't curse and didn't believe in "noisy coaching," although he could when he wanted to make a point understood very forcefully. He preferred to use a set lineup and employed his bench players only when the situation warranted.

Since Mack had to balance the team's financial books as well as direct operations on the field, the Athletics had their ups and downs over the years. More than once he was forced to break up a good team and suffer the consequences in the standings, as he did after the 1914 season, when he could no longer afford to pay players what they demanded in light of the Federal League challenge. He was formal and courtly in speech. While Bender, his Chippewa Indian pitcher was called "Chief" by everyone else, Mack always addressed him as Albert. One can hope that he made an exception for Stuffy, who much preferred that to Jack or John. In his early years with the Athletics, Mack won six American League championships— the first in 1902, when Rube Waddell was his ace pitcher, before the National League recognized the upstarts as fellow major leaguers — and four in five years during the Stuffy McInnis era. After he broke up his great team following 1914, the A's hit the skids for a decade before he began to build another winner, leading up to three consecutive pennants and two World Series titles in 1929-31. Then economic conditions resulting from the Great Depression forced him to sell off his stars again; after 1933 he would only once finish in the first division, and that was fourth place. Five times he managed World Series winners. His overall managerial record was 3,731 wins and 3,948 losses, both records of course. When in 1905 John McGraw of the Giants sarcastically compared the Athletics to "a big white elephant," Mack adopted a white elephant as the team's official logo, still used more than a century later. He treasured intelligence in his players as well as hustle, which was one reason he was so fond of Stuffy and Eddie Collins. Mack got rid of young "Shoeless" Joe Jackson, the unlettered country boy who might have had the finest natural batting stroke ever, because despite his talent the manager couldn't abide Jackson's attitude and sometimes unintelligent play. In Jackson's defense, some of the Athletics made him sullen by taunting him for his illiteracy. Over the course of his career, Mack said he had seen too many players squander their ability through their fondness for alcohol, which was why he didn't want his boys to drink. A *Wikipedia* article quoting "The Bill James Guide to Baseball Managers" said that "Mack looked for seven things in a young player: physical ability, intelligence, courage, disposition, will power, general alertness and personal habits." It is easy to see why he was so fond of young Stuffy McInnis.

And despite his overwhelming love for the game of baseball, Mack had to consider the business aspect of the sport at a time when there was no television revenue and gate receipts were the main source of income.

He loved to win, but when a team was often on the edge of financial trouble, winning didn't always pay. A quote often attributed to Mack sums up the conflict he often must have felt. "It is more profitable for me to have a team that is in contention for most of the season but finishes about fourth. A team like that will draw well enough during the first part of the season to show a profit for the year, and you don't have to give the players raises when they don't win." After three last place finishes, he traded Stuffy McInnis when the first baseman refused to accept a pay cut for 1918.

Over the last 16 years of his managing career, the old master seemed to have increasing difficulty keeping up with what was a rapidly changing game. But even after he entered his 80s, he never gave a thought to giving up his seat in the dugout. By the late 1940s he did agree to bring in Jimmy Dykes to help by being what was in effect baseball's first "bench coach." Today's big league managers usually employ such a top aide, but it was unusual back then. Three of Connie's sons, Roy and Earle from his first marriage and Connie Jr. from his second, became involved in the team's front office operations and assumed increasing control. The "Tall Tactician's" final season in the dugout, his 50th, was 1950, when he was 87. By then he was relying more and more on Dykes, and to some of the younger players he was just a silly old man who occasionally nodded off in the late innings of a one-sided game. That year the attention of Philadelphia baseball fans was turned almost entirely to the youthful Phillies, known as the "Whiz Kids," who became the talk of baseball when they captured the National League pennant. (They turned out to be one-year wonders.) The Athletics finished a dismal eighth in 1950, winning 52 games while losing 102. After that season, the Mack sons insisted that their father retire and let Dykes take over as manager.

The next spring must have been hard indeed for the old man. Sadly, he would live until Feb. 8, 1956, long enough to see his beloved Athletics sold to Arnold Johnson, who in 1955 transferred the team to Kansas City. Like the double hand-off of the Braves from Boston to Milwaukee and then on to Atlanta, Johnson turned the A's over to Charles O. Finley, who moved them to Oakland where in the 1970s new glory awaited the franchise under Manager Dick Williams, former skipper of the Red Sox. Kansas City would get the expansion Royals, and Philadelphia, like Boston, remained a one-team town. But the legacy of Connie Mack is the legendary impact he made on the great sport of baseball. It's a sure thing that the sport will never see anyone like him again.

ILLUSTRATIONS

No photo of Peabody's Field in Beverly has been located. This 1907 city map shows where the field was, and includes a structure labeled "Grand Stand." The ballpark was demolished in 1909 for a housing development.

(Beverly Historical Society)

We have found no pictorial record of Dick Madden's semi-pro team of the early 20th century. This unlabeled and undated photo from that time period is a definite possibility. If so, Madden might be the stocky man fourth from the right in the second row. And the diminutive, youthful-looking player second from the right in that row bears a decided facial resemblance to the drawing of Stuffy in his "rookie" baseball card.   (Beverly Historical Society)

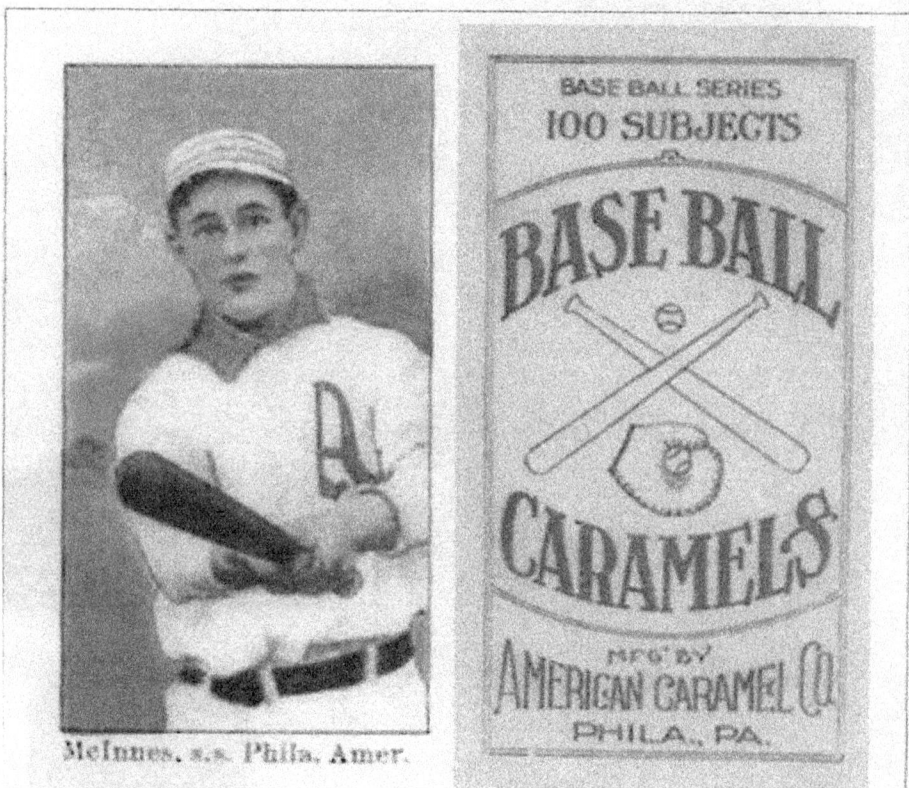

The American Caramel Co. sponsored early sets of major league player cards. Here is Stuffy in a Philadelphia Athletics uniform in 1909, when he was an 18-year-old rookie on Connie Mack's team. Note that his last name is misspelled; he was so new that the card writer couldn't get it right. (Private Collection)

This post card photo shows a young Stuffy in a Philadelphia Athletics uniform
(Beverly Historical Society)

Stuffy 's teammates in the "100,000 Infield" were Eddie Collins, left, second base; Jack Barry, shortstop; and Frank "Home Run" Baker, third base. (Public Domain)

The great Hall of Famer Connie Mack, owner of the Philadelphia Athletics and the team's field manager for in incredible 50 seasons. Mack took Dick Madden's advice and signed Stuffy, made him the regular first baseman in 1911, and traded him to Boston in 1918.   (Public Domain)

Stuffy, probably at the time he was with Boston Red Sox, for whom he played four seasons.   (Beverly Historical Society)

STUFFY McINNIS
BOSTON BRAVES – 1ST BASE   1923

Here's Stuffy with the Boston Braves in 1923. He signed with the National League team after being released by the Cleveland Indians, with whom he had set a new major league fielding record in 1922.   (Beverly Historical Society)

Stuffy's last World Series appearance came in 1925 for the Pittsburgh Pirates, in whose uniform he is shown here. After sitting out the first four games, Stuffy, came off the bench to lead the Pirates to a comeback seven-game triumph over the Washington Senators. It was his 17th season as a big league ballplayer, and he was 35 years old when the season ended   (Public Domain)

The Bridge Street Grounds in Salem, Mass., where Stuffy's minor professional Salem Witches of the New England League played in 1927. (Nelson Dionne)

The house on Tappan Street in Manchester built for Stuffy and Elsie (Dow) McInnis when they were married in 1918. They lived there for the rest of their lives.   (Ed Brown)

BEVERLY,	AB	B	PO	A	E
Hafford, cf	4	0	3	0	0
Barnes, lf	5	0	1	0	1
Orcott, ss	3	2	2	1	1
Mathews, c	4	3	6	1	1
Reynolds, 1b	5	3	10	1	0
Nesbit, 3b	4	2	2	0	1
Grant, rf	5	1	0	0	0
McInnis, 2b	5	1	1	6	0
McRae, p	3	0	2	3	0
Totals,	38	12	27	12	4

NEWTOWNE,	AB	B	PO	A	E
White, ss	5	2	1	0	2
Yeager, 3b	5	2	2	1	0
Pote, lf	5	3	2	0	1
Clarkson, 1b	4	0	9	1	1
Pickard, cf	2	0	2	1	0
Brown, rf	3	0	0	0	1
Carlisle, c	4	0	6	2	2
Rogers, 2b	4	1	2	5	1
Hannum, p	2	0	0	4	2
Totals,	34	8	24	14	10

Innings,	1	2	3	4	5	6	7	8	9	
Beverly,	0	1	3	0	1	4	0	3	0	—12
Newtowne,	0	0	1	0	0	0	0	1	3	— 5

Runs (by whom made)—Hafford, Orcott 2, Matthews 4, Reynolds 2, Nesbit 2, McRae; White, Yeager, Rogers 2, Hannum. Two base hits —Mathews 2, Nesbit, Grant, McInnis, Pote. Sacrifice hits—Grant, Clarkson, Hannum, White, Reynolds. Stolen bases—Mathews, Nesbit 3, McRae, Rogers. First base on balls —Off McRae 4; off Hannum 4. Struck out—By McRae 4; by Hannum 4. Passed ball—Carlisle. Wild pitches—Hannum. Hit by pitched ball—Hafford, Rogers. Time—1 hour, 44 minutes. Umpire—Gorman.

In the Sunday School league: Dane Street 5, North Beverly 2. Universalists 24, Wenham 10. Hamilton 11, Baptist 8.

CRICKET

The result of Saturday's game was a defeat of the home team.

CARRIBEAN C. C.

T. Chambers, b Potter........... 0

This May 1907 newspaper box score might be from Stuffy's first game for Beverly when the Madden men defeated "Newtowne" 12-5 at Peabody's Field. Stuffy had a hit that day and sparkled at second base, leading to shouts of "That's the stuff, Kid!" The visitors did not exactly play sterling defensive baseball, judging from the 10 errors charged to Newtowne.

(Beverly Historical Society)

STUFFY McINNIS 191

John Phalen "Jack" McInnis
Height: 5'9.5"   Weight: 162   Bats: Right   Throws: Right
Born: Sep. 19, 1890, Gloucester, MA
Died: Feb. 16, 1960, Ipswich, MA

YEAR	TEAM	G	AB	R	H	2B	3B	HR	RBI	AVG
1909	Phi-A	19	46	4	11	0	0	1	4	.239
1910	Phi-A	38	73	10	22	2	4	0	12	.301
1911	Phi-A	126	468	76	150	20	10	3	77	.321
1912	Phi-A	153	568	83	186	25	13	3	101	.327
1913	Phi-A	148	543	79	176	30	4	4	90	.324
1914	Phi-A	149	576	74	181	12	8	1	95	.314
1915	Phi-A	119	456	44	143	14	4	0	49	.314
1916	Phi-A	140	512	42	151	25	3	1	60	.295
1917	Phi-A	150	567	50	172	19	4	0	44	.303
1918	Bos-A	117	423	40	115	11	5	0	56	.272
1919	Bos-A	120	440	32	134	12	5	1	58	.305
1920	Bos-A	148	559	50	166	21	3	2	71	.297
1921	Bos-A	152	584	72	179	31	10	0	76	.307
1922	Cle-A	142	537	58	164	28	7	1	78	.305
1923	Bos-N	154	607	70	191	23	9	2	95	.315
1924	Bos-N	146	581	57	169	23	7	1	59	.291
1925	Pit-N	59	155	19	57	10	4	0	24	.368
1926	Pit-N	47	127	12	38	6	1	0	13	.299
1927	Phi-N	1	0	0	0	0	0	0	0	—
TOTAL		2128	7822	872	2405	312	101	20	1062	.307

One of the best fielding first basemen in history, "Stuffy" McInnis' 20,119 lifetime putouts is 5th on the all-time list. He hit .307 with 2,405 career hits and played in 5 World Series.

The Sporting News ®
CONLON COLLECTION®

Stuffy's lifetime career batting statistics, compiled by the *The Sporting News*. (Beverly Historical Society)

BIBLIOGRAPHY

Abbott, Gordon, Jeffrey's Creek, Manchester, Mass. Historical Society, 2003.

Anderson, Will, The Lost New England Nine, Bath, Maine, Anderson and Sons Publishing Co., 2003.

Durant, John, The Story of Baseball, New York, Hastings House, 1947.

Gay, Timothy M., Tris Speaker, Rough and Tumble Life of a Baseball Legend, University of Nebraska Press, 2006.

Huhn, Rick, The Sizzler, Missouri University Press, 2004

Lieb, Frederick G., The Boston Red Sox, New York, G. F. Putnam's Sons, 1947.

Macht, Norman Lee, Connie Mack and the Early Years of Baseball, Copyright by Author, 2007.

Rice, Grantland, The Tumult and the Shouting, New York, A.S. Barnes & Company, 1954.

Shatzkin, Mike, ed., The Ballplayers, New York, Arbor House William Morrow, 1990.

Ward, Geoffrey C. and Burns, Ken, Baseball, New York, Alfred A. Knoff, 1994.

Baseball Biography Project, The Society for American Baseball Research, 2009.

Beverly City Documents, 1906, 1908.

Harvard Crimson, various issues, 1948, 1949, 1950, 1952.

Information provided by Anthony Mariano, Director of Athletics, Norwich University

Material on file at the Beverly Historical Society and Museum, where the author is a volunteer researcher

Material from the Philadelphia Athletics Historical Society, Hatboro, Pa.

Newspapers, various issues: New York Times, Beverly Evening Times, Salem (Evening) News, Beverly Citizen, (Beverly) Saturday Morning Citizen, Manchester Cricket, Boston Globe, Gloucester Times.

North Shore Golf magazine, August-September 2009.

On-line sources: The Baseball Nexus, Wikipedia, Baseball-Reference.com, Baseball-library.com, BaseballAlmanac.com, MLB.com, Program History, Amherst College

Personal recollections of John C. Burke, Constance Brown, Richard Littlefield and Mary Mahoney

"Play Hard, Play Fast, Play Ball," Nova Scotia Sports Hall of Fame, Halifax.

Various municipal directories for Beverly, Manchester, Wenham and Hamilton, published by Crowley & Lunt.

Notes in the author's personal files

ABOUT THE AUTHOR

Edward "Ed" Brown is a retired newspaper writer, editor and columnist. In retirement he is a volunteer and a past Trustee for the Beverly Historical Society, with a special interest in the Rev. John Hale House. He is the author of two local history books, "Thieves, Cowbeaters and Other True Tales of Colonial Beverly," and "What Only Two Could Do," the story of Beverly native Frederick Lincoln Ashworth's vital role in the delivery of the atomic bomb on Japan in 1945. Ed has also written several history-themed booklets including "Beverly Bedeviled," a collection of Beverly connections to the Salem Witchcraft Trials; and "Guardian of the Flame," the story of Hospital Point lighthouse keeper Joseph Henry Herrick. All are available for purchase through the Beverly Historical Society.

A Beverly native, Ed is a Boston University graduate and a U.S. Army veteran who served overseas with the Army Security Agency in Sinop, Turkey. He's a third generation Society volunteer, following his mother and grandfather. He's also active in his church and a local American Legion post. His favorite sport is baseball and his favorite season is summer.

www.ingramcontent.com/pod-product-compliance
Lightning Source LLC
LaVergne TN
LVHW091309080426
835510LV00007B/428